"Dogs are our link to paradise...to sit with a dog on a hillside on a glorious afternoon is to be back in Eden, where doing nothing was not boring - it was peace."

- Milan Kundera

Contents

Also...

Introduction

The Philadelphia region can be a great place to hike with your dog. Within an hour's drive you can hike on sand trails, climb hills that leave you panting, walk on some of the most historic grounds in America, explore the estates of America's wealthiest families or circle lakes for 7 miles and never lose sight of the water.

This is the second edition of A BARK IN THE PARK - THE 55 BEST PLACES TO HIKE WITH YOUR DOG IN THE PHILA-DELPHIA REGION. The book still features more than 100 such places within 50 miles of Philadelphia's City Hall where you can hike with your dog. I have selected what I consider to be the 55 best places to take the dog and ranked them according to subjective criteria including the variety of hikes available, opportunities for canine swimming and pleasure of the walks. The rankings include a mix of parks that feature long walks and parks that contain short walks. I have also included another 63 places to walk the dog.

I have added some new hikes and included four regional hikes - one to the east, one to the west, one to the north, one to the south - all canine hikers will want to try. I have also reviewed and ranked the Delaware Valley's dog parks.

For dog owners it is important to realize that not all parks are open to our four-legged friends (see page 136 for a list of parks that do not allow dogs). It is sometimes hard for we dog owners to believe but not everyone loves dogs. We are, in fact, in the minority when compared with our non-dog owning neigbors. So when visiting a park always keep your dog under control and clean up any messes and we can all expect our great parks to remain open to our dogs. So grab that leash and hit the trail!
DBG

Hiking With Your Dog

So you want to start hiking with your dog. Hiking with your dog can be a fascinating way to explore the Philadelphia region from a canine perspective. Some things to consider:

🐾 Dog's Health

Hiking can be a wonderful preventative for any number of physical and behavioral disorders. One in every three dogs is overweight and running up trails and leaping through streams is great exercise to help keep pounds off. Hiking can also relieve boredom in a dog's routine and calm dogs prone to destructive habits. And hiking with your dog strengthens the overall owner/dog bond.

🐾 Breed of Dog

All dogs enjoy the new scents and sights of a trail. But some dogs are better suited to hiking than others. If you don't as yet have a hiking companion, select a breed that matches your interests. Do you look forward to an entire afternoon's hiking? You'll need a dog bred to keep up with such a pace, such as a retriever or a spaniel. Is a half-hour enough walking for you? It may not be for an energetic dog like a border collie. If you already have a hiking friend, tailor your plans to his abilities.

🐾 Conditioning

Just like humans, dogs need to be acclimated to the task at hand. An inactive dog cannot be expected to bounce from the easy chair in the den to complete a 3-hour hike. You must also be physically able to restrain your dog if confronted with distractions on the trail (like a scampering squirrel or a pack of joggers). Have your dog checked by a veterinarian before significantly increasing your dog's activity level.

🐾 Weather

Hot humid summers do not do dogs any favors. With no sweat glands and only panting available to disperse body heat, dogs are much more susceptible to heat stroke than we are. Unusually rapid panting and/or a bright red tongue are signs of heat exhaustion in your pet. Always carry enough water for your hike. Even days that don't seem too warm can cause discomfort in dark-coated dogs if the sun is shining brightly. In cold weather, short-coated breeds may require additional attention.

🐾 Trail Hazards

Dogs won't get poison ivy but they can transfer it to you. Stinging nettle is a nuisance plant that lurks on the side of many trails and the slightest brush will deliver troublesome needles into a dog's coat. Some trails are littered with small pieces of broken glass that can slice a dog's paws. Nasty thorns can also blanket trails that we in shoes may never notice.

🐾 Ticks

You won't be able to visit any of the Philadelphia region's parks without encountering ticks. All are nasty but the deer tick - no bigger than a pin head - carries with it the spectre of lyme disease. In 1999 Pennsylvania ranked third among all states in the number of cases of lyme disease reported,

New Jersey fourth and Delaware tenth. Lyme disease attacks a dog's joints and makes walking painful. The tick needs to be embedded in the skin to transmit lyme disease. It takes 4-6 hours for a tick to become embedded and another 24-48 hours to transmit lyme disease bacteria.

When hiking, walk in the middle of trails away from tall grass and bushes. If your walk includes fields, consider long sleeves and long pants tucked into high socks. Wear a hat - ticks like hair. By checking your dog - and yourself - thoroughly after each walk you can help avoid lyme disease. Ticks tend to congregate on your dog's ears, between the toes and around the neck and head.

❧ Water

Surface water, including fast-flowing streams, is likely to be infested with a microscopic protozoa called *Giardia*, waiting to wreak havoc on your dog's intestinal system. The most common symptom is potentially crippling diarrhea. Algae, pollutants and contaminants can all be in streams, ponds and puddles. If possible, carry fresh water for your dog on the trail - your dog can even learn to drink happily from a squirt bottle.

I can't think of anything that brings me closer to tears than when my old dog - completely exhausted after a hard day in the field - limps away from her nice spot in front of the fire and comes over to where I'm sitting and puts her head in my lap, a paw over my knee, and closes her eyes, and goes back to sleep. I don't know what I've done to deserve that kind of friend."
-Gene Hill

Outfitting Your Dog For A Hike

These are the basics for taking your dog on a hike:

▸ **Collar.**   It should not be so loose as to come off but you should be able to slide your flat hand under the collar.

▸ **Identification Tags**.   Get one with your veterinarian's phone number as well.

▸ **Bandanna**.   Can help distinguish him from game in hunting season.

▸ **Leash**.   Leather lasts forever but if there's water in your future, consider quick-drying nylon.

▸ **Water**.   Carry 8 ounces for every hour of hiking.

🐾   *I want my dog to help carry water, snacks and other supplies on the trail. Where do I start?*
To select an appropriate dog pack. Measure your dog's girth around the rib cage to determine the best pack size. A dog pack should fit securely without hindering the dog's ability to walk normally.

🐾   *Will my dog wear a pack?*
Wearing a dog pack is no more obtrusive than wearing a collar, although some dogs will take to a pack easier than others. Introduce the pack by draping a towel over your dog's back in the house and then having your dog wear an empty pack on short walks. Progressively add some crumpled newspaper and then bits of clothing. Fill the pack with treats and reward your dog from the stash. Soon your dog will associate the dog pack with an outdoor adventure and will eagerly look forward to wearing it.

How much weight can I put into a dog pack?

Many dog packs are sold by weight recommendations. A healthy, well-conditioned dog can comfortably carry 25% to 33% of its body weight. Breeds prone to back problems or hip dysplasia should not wear dog packs. Consult your veterinarian before stuffing the pouches with gear.

How does a dog wear a pack?

The pack, typically with cargo pouches on either side, should ride as close to the shoulders as possible without limiting movement. The straps that hold the dog pack in place should be situated where they will not cause chafing.

What are good things to put in a dog pack?

Low density items such as food and poop bags are good choices. Ice cold bottles of water can cool your dog down on hot days. Don't put anything in a dog pack that can break. Dogs will bang the pack on rocks and trees as they wiggle through tight spots in the trail. Dogs also like to lie down in creeks and other wet spots so seal items in plastic bags. A good use for dog packs when on day hikes around Philadelphia is trail maintenance - your dog can pack out trash left by inconsiderate visitors before you.

🐾   *Are dog booties a good idea?*

Dog booties can be an asset, especially for the occasional canine hiker whose paw pads have not become toughened. Many of the trails near Philadelphia involve rocky terrain. In some places, broken glass abounds. Hiking boots for dogs are designed to prevent pads from cracking while trotting across rough surfaces. Used in winter, dog booties provide warmth and keep ice balls from forming between toe pads when hiking through snow.

🐾   *What should a doggie first aid kit include?*

Even when taking short hikes it is a good idea to have some basics available for emergencies:

- ▸ 4" square gauze pads
- ▸ cling type bandaging tapes
- ▸ topical wound disinfectant cream
- ▸ tweezers
- ▸ petroleum jelly (to cover ticks)
- ▸ veterinarian's phone number

"We are alone, absolutely alone on this chance planet; and, amid all the forms of life that surround us, not one, excepting the dog, has made an alliance with us."
-Maurice Maeterlinck

Low Impact Hiking With Your Dog

Every time you hike with your dog on the trail you are an ambassador for all dog owners. Some people you meet won't believe in your right to take a dog on the trail. Be friendly to all and make the best impression you can by practicing low impact hiking with your dog:

- Pack out everything you pack in.

- Do not leave dog scat on the trail; if you haven't brought plastic bags for poop removal bury it away from the trail and topical water sources.

- Hike only where dogs are allowed.

- Stay on the trail.

- Do not allow your dog to chase wildlife.

- Step off the trail and wait with your dog while horses and other hikers pass.

- Do not allow your dog to bark - people are enjoying the trail for serenity.

- Have as much fun on your hike as your dog does.

The Other End Of The Leash

Leash laws are like speed limits - everyone seems to have a private interpretation of their validity. Some dog owners never go outside with an unleashed dog; others treat the laws as suggestions or disregard them completely. It is not the purpose of this book to tell dog owners where to go to evade the leash laws or reveal the parks where rangers will look the other way at an unleashed dog. Nor is it the business of this book to preach vigilant adherence to the leash laws. Nothing written in a book is going to change people's behavior with regard to leash laws. So this will be the last time leash laws are mentioned, save occasionally when we point out the parks where dogs are welcomed off leash.

"No one appreciates the very special genius of your conversation as a dog does."
-Christopher Morley

The Best of the Best...

The 10 Best Places To Hike With Your Dog
In the Philadelphia Region

Blue Ribbon - French Creek State Park

Approximately 40 miles of trails visit every corner of French Creek's 7,339 acres. There are nine featured hikes on wide dirt paths of between one and four hours' duration. The marquee walk is the *Boone Trail*, a six-mile loop connecting all the major attractions of the park. Two large lakes make first rate canine swimming holes.

#2 - Andorra Natural Area/Fairmount Park

America's first public park and home of the Philadelphia Art Museum, is the largest contiguous landscaped municipal park in the world, sprawling across nearly 9,000 acres. It is the bucolic home to an estimated 2,500,000 trees and on weekend mornings it can seem as if there is a dog for every one. If the communal dog walking on Forbidden Drive isn't for you, take to the hills and try the extensive trail system up the slopes of Wissahickon Gorge.

#3 - Valley Forge National Historic Park

These are some of the most historic walks in America and some of the most beautiful in greater Philadelphia - panoramic vistas from rolling hills, long waterside hikes and climbs up wooded mountainsides. If you're not up to mingling with the tourists, cross the Schuylkill River and try the 3-mile linear *Schuylkill River Trail* that connects the Pawling's Parking Area and the Betzwood Picnic Area. The flat dirt trail hugs the river the entire way. Dogs are welcome throughout the historic park.

The unmarked trails in Valley Forge's Walnut Section don't appear on park maps and are missed by most visitors.

#4 - White Clay Creek State Park/Preserve

The Lenni Lenape recognized the great beauty of the White Clay Creek and made their most important "Indian Town" along its banks. There are eight marked trails at White Clay Creek, a state park in Delaware and a state preserve in Pennsylvania. The *Penndel Trail* connects the two as it traces the meanderings of the stream. If you can't get enough of the great hiking with your dog here, two new tracts of land have recently opened nearby under the administration of White Clay Creek State Park.

#5 - Scott Arboretum
Several area colleges welcome responsible dog owners - Swarthmore's Scott Arboretum is the best walk. The collections are integrated with the stone buildings of the college which dates to 1864. Leaving the cultivated plantings of the campus, a variety of hillside trails lead through the 200-acre Crum Woods down to Crum Creek. Dogs are not only welcomed at Swarthmore, but there are water bowls chained to some of the drinking fountains. In the Crum Woods your dog need only be under voice control, not leashed.

#6 - Woodlawn Trustees Property
Adjacent to the popular Brandywine Creek State Park (with 8 trails and 14 miles of hiking of its own) are more than 2,000 acres open to the public for hiking and riding. Miles of informal trails can be combined to create any kind of day out with your dog. Athletic dogs will enjoy romping across the grassy hills above the Brandywine Creek. Walking back and forth on the *Fire Trail* along the water provides an easy 45-minute stroll. The Woodlawn trails serve up as fine a mix of open meadow and mature woodlands hiking as you're likely to find in greater Philadelphia.

#7 - Green Lane Park
Dogs are not allowed on the *Hemlock Point Trail* but there is plenty of rich canine hiking on the park's other four trails to set tails to wagging. The *Red Trail*, designed as an equestrian trail but not chewed up like so many other such surfaces, winds through open fields and stands of trees for 10 miles, although the entire length can be aborted in several places. The premier trail at Green Lane Park is the heavily wooded *Blue Trail* on the western edge of the reservoir where you pick your way across steep ravines and narrow ridges for 6 miles.

#8 - Ridley Creek State Park

The park chains water bowls around its benches along the *Multi-Use Trail* and your dog will welcome the cool drink after tackling the 12 miles of hilly Ridley Creek State Park trails. If the park's four main blazed trails don't tire her out try an unmarked trailhead just east of Ridley Creek on Gradyville Road offers one of the longest creekside walks in Delaware County.

#9 - Fair Hill Natural Area

Located just across the Delaware state line in Maryland, this is the Godzilla of area hiking. Traversing its 5,613 acres are over 75 miles of multi-use trails. Fair Hill was a horse farm formerly owned by sportsman William du Pont, Jr. and was one of the largest private land holdings on the East Coast. The trails through the fields are typically double-track (old dirt vehicle roads), although singletrack trails dominate in the forested areas. Many roll through golden hayfields as befits Fair Hill's stature as a leading equine training center.

#10 - Wharton State Forest

Wharton State Forest lies at the heart of New Jersey's mysterious Pine Barrens, a tapestry of impenetrable scrub pine, swamps and bogs that is the stomping ground of the notorious Jersey Devil. The main pathway is the *Batona Trail*, a 49-mile pink-blazed wilderness trail that begins at Ongs Hat in the north and ends at Lake Absegami in Bass River State Forest to the south. The hard-packed sand trail, that sports some gentle undulations to break up a mostly flat walk, is a joy under paw and boot. The Batsto River flowing through the forest is stained the color of tea by cedar sap, adding to the region's mystique. It makes an excellent canine swimming pool.

10 Cool Things To See On Philadelphia Region Trails With Your Dog

"If your dog is fat," the old saying goes, "you aren't getting enough exercise." But walking the dog need not be just about a little exercise. Here are 10 cool things you can see in the Philadelphia region while out walking the dog.

❧ FOLK ART

In 1855, a hotel entrepreneur built a new inn on Rex Avenue. To draw attention to his hostelry he constructed an Indian from old barn boards and propped it up on top of a rock overlooking the Gorge. In 1902, when the Indian Rock Hotel was long gone but with the silhouette still there, artist Massey Rhind was commissioned to make a representation of a "Delaware Indian, looking west to where his people have gone." The kneeling warrior has gazed up the Wissahickon Gorge ever since. A switchback trail in **Fairmount Park** leads to the Indian Statue where you can get close enough to pat his knee. And take in a breath-abducting view.

🐾 MONUMENTAL MONUMENTS

The *Multi-Use Trail* at **Valley Forge National Historic Park rolls** past reconstructed huts and parade grounds that transport you back to the Revolution. The National Memorial Arch, a massive stone tribute dedicated in 1917, stands out along the route. The inscription reads: "Naked and starving as they are, we cannot enough admire the incomparable patience and fidelity of the soldiery. Washington at Valley Forge, February 16, 1778." In the southern part of **White Clay Creek State Park/Preserve**, reached by the *Twin Valley Trail*, is the Arc Corner Monument marking one end of the 12-mile arc that forms the Pennsylvania-Delaware state line, unique in American political boundary-making. The circular divide dates to William Penn's directive of August 28, 1701, when Delaware was still a part of Pennsylvania, known as the Lower Three Counties. A little more than 1/2 mile to the west is another monument marking the tri-state junction of Delaware, Maryland and Pennsylvania.

🐾 AMERICAN CASTLES

While on the trails on the **Woodlawn Trustees Property** several times you will break out of the woods to views of a spectacular home on a neighboring hill. It is Granogue, one of the ancestral duPont family homes in the Brandywine Valley. You hike past another at **Bellevue State Park.** Other historic mansions you can view up close with your dog are Fonthill at **Fonthill**, Oakbourne at **Oakbourne Park**, the Curtis estate in **Curtis Park** and the Swayne Mansion in **Hibernia County Park**.

🐾 MOVIE LOCATIONS

Flying concentric circles outward from Philadelphia, Hollywood location scouts for Oprah Winfrey's movie project, *Beloved*, spotted the **Fair Hill Natural Area** terrain and selected it as the backdrop for the film's rural scenes. A ramshackle 19th-century tenant farm was constructed and much of the movie shot here. The producers decided to leave the movie set intact, to deteriorate naturally. You can wander among the fake buildings and even knock on the styrofoam stones.

❖ REMARKABLE BRIDGES

In the farthest northern section of **Tyler State Park** is the longest covered bridge in Bucks County. The 117-year old Schofield Ford Covered Bridge burned in 1991 but after five years of fundraising the 166-foot, two-span crossing was entirely rebuilt by volunteers on its original stone abutments using authentic period materials and methods. An elaborate, reinforced wooden railroad trestle bridges a ravine on the *Glen Trail* in the **Wenonah Woods**. The trail runs by a stream under the trestle and there are sweeping views from the top. A walk through **Brandywine Park** provides a quick lesson in the history of bridge architecture. The classical arch form is represented in grand style with the

magnificent stone viaduct across the river and numerous reinforced concrete spans. There is even a small iron arch bridge over the mill race. A prototypical 19th century pier and girder iron bridge transports trains over the Brandy-wine. And the pedestrian footbridge across the water, the Swinging Bridge, is a little suspension bridge employing the same engineering principles as the mythical Brooklyn Bridge. Along the *Paper Mill Trail* in the **Pennypack Preserve**, just off the *Creek Road Trail*, is a stone double-arch bridge built in 1847. In what is now **Pennypack Park**, William Penn asked in 1683 that "an order be given for building a bridge over the Pennypack." Designated a National Civil Engineering Landmark, the first Three Arch Stone Bridge is the oldest stone bridge still carrying heavy traffic in America.

In 1850 Albert Fink, a German railroad engineer, designed and patented a bridge that used a latticework of rods instead of cables to reinforce stiffness. This construction was cheap and sturdy, making the Fink Truss one of the most commonly used railroad bridges in the 1860s, especially favored by the powerful Baltimore & Ohio Railroad. Only one Fink Truss bridge remains in the United States - an abandoned 108-foot span in Zoarsville, Ohio. A wooden reproduction of a Fink Truss is in a field at **Warwick County Park** for you and your dog to climb.

🐾 IMPRESSIVE FORTS

Where else can a dog climb into an actual battery and scan the Delaware River where gunnery officers once aimed guns capable of accurately firing 1,000-pound projectiles eight miles like he can at **Fort Mott State Park**? Fort DuPont, named for Civil War fleet commander Admiral Samuel Francis duPont and now a Delaware state park, saw active duty in three wars before becoming a state park. The 1-mile *River View Trail*, a grassy loop path, begins in the marshland along the Delaware River and finishes in shaded woodlands. The trail takes you past several ruins of the military installation, camoflauged to river traffic, and features sustained views of the Delaware River and Fort Delaware on Pea Patch Island.

🐾 CANAL LOCKS

Pennsylvania's first canal system was cobbled together in 1815 using 120 locks to stretch 108 miles from the coal fields of Schuylkill County to Philadelphia. Railroads began chewing away at canal business in the 1860s and the last coal barges floated down the Schuylkill River in the 1920s. Today, the only sections of the canal in existence are at Manayunk and Lock 60, built by area name donor Thomas Oakes, at the **Schuylkill Canal Park**. In 1985 the Schuylkill Canal Association formed to keep the canal flowing and maintain the lock and towpath. In 1988, the area was added to the National Register of Historic Places. The Delaware Canal State Park features a strolling towpath that runs for 60 miles north of Bristol to Easton.

🐾 CHAMPION TREES

The **Taylor Memorial Arboretum** provides a 12-Tree Self-Guided Tour. The collection is especially strong in Far Eastern specimens and spotlights three Pennsylvania State Champion trees: the Needle Juniper, the Lacebark Elm and the Giant Dogwood. Also on the tour is a Dawn Redwood, an ancient tree known only through fossils until 1941 when a botany student tracked down living specimens in rural China. Some of the first seed to come to America resulted in this tree. Liberated from their sun-stealing neighbors of the crowded woods in **Springton Manor Park**, the "King" and "Queen" White Oaks have spread out into a massive canopy of leaves. The "Queen" measures seventeen feet around at the thickest part of the trunk and the "King" is closer to twenty. The two trees are part of the "Penn's Woods" collection of 139 trees standing when William Penn arrived to survey his Pennsylvania colony. The arboreal oldsters reside at the last stop of the park's *Nature Trail*. Awbury Arboretum in East Germantown was the summer estate of 19th century Quaker shipping merchant Henry Cope. Across the 55 acres are plantings of groves and clusters of trees set amidst large swaths of grass fields in the English landscape garden tradition. You can investigate more than 200 species, mostly native, in your informal explorations of the grounds. Old macadam paths lead to most areas of the odd-shaped property. Also on the grounds are wetlands surrounding an artificial pond.

🐾 RUSTIC BARNS

While many of the Hospital Farm's buildings have disappeared in **Norristown Farm Park**, the unique dairy barn remains. Built in 1914, it is shaped like a wheel with four spokes. In 1961 alone, nine cows produced 1.1 million pounds of milk - more than 300 pounds of milk per cow per day. At the **Riverbend Education Center** the Visitor Center is a restoration of a 1923 Sears & Roebuck mail order barn. A century ago Sears sold anything and everything by mail- including kits for building houses and barns. The kit, which could cost as little as a few hundred dollars depending on style, would include rough lumber, framing timbers, plank flooring, shingles, hardware, sash and paint. Usually shipped by train from the west, the barn kit would be loaded onto a freight wagon and hauled to the building site for assembly by local carpenters.

And our vote for the coolest thing of all on Philadelphia trails...

🐾 MUSICAL ROCKS

In a boulder field of volcanic rocks in **Ringing Rocks Park** are stones whose metallic bands stressed by several ice ages produce a ringing sound when struck by a metal object. Short, wide trails lead through the woods to the boulder field where you can mystify your dog by pounding on rocks with a hammer. Musical rocks ping while others just thud on "dead " spots.

Your dog will delight in the music you can make in Ringing Rocks Park.

The 55 Best Places To Hike With Your Dog In The Philadelphia Region...

1
French Creek State Park

The Park

A wilderness fort once stood on the small stream flowing through these woods that was garrisoned by the French during the French and Indian War and thus "French Creek." The hillsides here were dotted with charcoal hearths throughout the 1800s, fueling the nascent American iron industry. The furnace was stoked for the last time in 1883.

French Creek State Park was originally developed by the federal government during the Depression as a National Park Service Demonstration Area. Civilian Conservation Corps members, organized by President Franklin Roosevelt, built dams, roads and other recreational trappings. These workers also began restoration of the Hopewell Furnace, today a National Historic Site through which several of the park's trails pass. In 1946, the area was transferred to the Commonwealth of Pennsylvania.

Chester County

Distance from Philadelphia
- 44 miles
Phone Number
- (610) 582-9680
Website
- www.dcnr.state.pa.us/
  stateparks/parks/w-clay.htm
Admission Fee
- None
Directions
- French Creek State Park is north of Elverson. From Route 23, take Route 345 North to the south entrance of the park. From the Pennsylvania Turnpike the park is 7 miles northeast of the Morgantown Interchange (Exit 22).

The Walks

Approximately 40 miles of trails visit every corner of French Creek's 7,339 acres. There are nine featured hikes of between one and four hours' duration. The marquee walk is the *Boone Trail*, a six-mile loop connecting all the major attractions of the park. The *Mill Creek Trail* is a back-country hike that visits Millers Point, a pile of large boulders where you and your dog can easily scramble to the top.

All the walks are heavily forested with hardwoods - keep an eye out for the ruins of the area's charcoal-burning past. Repeatedly timbered, there is little understory and the trails are almost universally wide and easy to walk. The park is hilly with the steepest - and rockiest - slopes blanketing the eastern section of French Creek.

Trail Sense. Any park administrator desiring to blaze a trail would do well to visit French Creek State Park. Detailed trail maps are also available.

Dog Friendliness

Dogs are welcome on all the trails but are not permitted in campsites or swimming areas.

Traffic

Despite its popularity, the sheer size and number of hikes available conspire to create long stretches of solitude, especially in the rugged eastern end of the park. Horses are restricted to the yellow-blazed *Horse-Shoe Trail* and mountain bikes are banned from many trails, including all trails south of Park Road.

Canine Swimming

There is easy access to two lakes, the 21-acre cold water Scotts Run Lake and the 63-acre Hopewell Lake.

Trail Time

More than an hour.

2

Andorra Natural Area / Fairmount Park

The Park

America's first public park began with 5 acres in 1812. Today, Fairmount Park is the largest contiguous landscaped municipal park in the world with nearly 9,000 acres. It is the bucolic home to an estimated 2,500,000 trees.

The Andorra Natural Area, at the park's northern boundary with Montgomery County, evolved from a 19th century private nursery. Ownership of the property dates to 1840 when Richard Wistar named it "Andorra" from a Moorish word meaning "hills covered with trees." One of those trees - a massive sycamore - grew right through an enclosed porch in the house of the nursery's chief plant propagator. The weakening sycamore was cut down in 1981 but the Tree House survives as the Andorra Visitor Center.

Philadelphia County

Distance from Philadelphia
- 6 miles
Phone Number
- (215) 685-9285
Website
- www.philaparks.org/wvnatand.htm
Admission Fee
- None
Directions
- Andorra is on Northwestern Avenue between Ridge Avenue and Germantown Avenue (Route 422).

The Walks

The main trail at Andorra is a 20-station *Nature Hike*. There are also a dozen other named trails that branch off this loop. The *Forbidden Drive* begins its 7-mile journey along the Wissahickon Creek to the Schuylkill River here. So named when it was closed to automobiles in the 1920s, your outing on the Forbidden Drive can be shortened by several bridges across the Wissahickon. A natural dirt trail rolls along the opposite bank to create hiking loops.

The best canine hiking comes on these dirt trails when you leave the paved Forbidden Drive and climb out of the gorge. These narrow ribbons of dirt crossing the hillsides are a dog's delight time and again.

Trail Sense: The paths are blazed and a map of Andorra is available. Mapboards explain the Forbidden Drive trail system.

Dog Friendliness

Dogs are welcome on Forbidden Drive in Fairmount Park. Carpenter Woods is a popular spot for dogs to congregate.

Traffic

For those seeking a communal dog walking experience, the bustling Forbidden Drive is the place. Those in search of solitary contemplation can take to the hillside trails of the Wissahickon Gorge, although watch out for mountain bikes.

Canine Swimming

The swimming is excellent in the Wissahickon Creek with many access points.

Trail Time

More than an hour.

3

Valley Forge National Historic Park

The Park

The most famous name in the American Revolution comes to us from a small iron forge built along Valley Creek in the 1740s. No battles were fought here, but during the winter of 1777-78, when Valley Forge grew to be the third largest city in America, hundreds of soldiers died from sickness and disease. America's attention was redirected to long-forgotten Valley Forge during a Centennial in 1878. Preservation efforts began with Washington's Headquarters and evolved into the National Park.

The Walks

These are some of the most historic walks in America and some of the most beautiful in greater Philadelphia - panoramic vistas from rolling hills, long waterside hikes and

Chester County

Distance from Philadelphia
  - 24 miles
Phone Number
  - (610) 783-1000
Website
  - www.nps.gov/vafo/
Admission Fee
  - None
Directions
  - The main park entrance is on Route 23 off Route 422. Parking for the Valley Creek Trail is on Route 252 (although the Foot Bridge is washed out as of this writing). To reach the Schuylkill River Trail, exit from Route 422 onto Trooper Road, make a left and continue back across Route 422 to the Betzwood Picnic Area or cross the Schuylkill River on Pawlings Road from Route 23 at the other end. Parking for trails here is on the right side across the bridge and also up the road at Walnut Hill.

climbs up wooded mountainsides. There are four marked trails, plus miles of unmarked hikes. The paved *Multi-Use Trail* loops the Colonial defensive lines and Grand Parade Ground and visits George Washington's headquarters. Sweeping field scenes are found all along the trail's six-mile length. The *Valley Creek Trail* is a flat, linear 1.2 mile walk along Valley Creek, past the Upper

Forge site. Near the Valley Creek is the eastern terminus of the 133-mile *Horse-Shoe Trail*; the journey to the *Appalachian Trail* in Hershey begins at the Artificer's Shops on Route 23. The Horse-Shoe Trail demands a steep and strenuous climb up Mount Misery, the natural southern defender of Washington's encampment. Across the Schuylkill River is the 3-mile linear *Schuylkill River Trail* connecting the Pawling's Parking Area and the Betzwood Picnic Area. The flat dirt trail hugs the river the entire way.

Trail Sense: A National Park Service map provides locations for the trails and does not indicate the variety of side trails available, especially from the Schuylkill River Trail.

Dog Friendliness

Dogs are welcome on all the trails here.

Traffic

Valley Forge is popular with dog walkers, cyclists and joggers but there is relief from the crowds at Valley Forge on the unmarked dirt trails at Walnut Hill across the Schuylkill River, off Pawlings Road.

Canine Swimming

Valley Creek is a delightful watering hole and the Schuylkill River is easily accessed for hard-core swimming canines.

Trail Time

More than an hour.

4

White Clay Creek State Park/Preserve

The Park

William Penn bought most of this land in 1683 from Lenni Lenape Chief Kekelappen, who was believed to have lived here in Opasiskunk, the most important of the region's "Indian Towns." Frequent flooding over the past three centuries has obliterated all evidence of this former large settlement.

In 1968 public recreation at White Clay Creek began life as a Delaware state park with 24 acres of land. In 1984 the DuPont Company donated the land that would become the 2,300-acre Delaware state park and the 1,253-acre Pennsylvania preserve.

The Walks

There are eight marked trails in White Clay Creek State Park. The top trails of the Walter S. Carpenter, Jr.

New Castle County

Distance from Philadelphia
- 37 miles
Phone Number
- (302) 368-6900
- (610) 255-5415
Website
- www.dnrec.state.de.us/ parkprograms/wccsp.htm
www.dcnr.state.pa.us/ stateparks/parks/w-clay.htm
Admission Fee
- None in the Preserve; an entrance fee is collected in Delaware during the summer season and on weekends and holidays in May, September and October.
Directions
- The White Clay Creek Valley is 3 miles north of Newark. A main entrance is on Route 896 and other parking areas can be reached via Route 896 on London Tract Road, Chambers Rock Road and Hopkins Road.

Recreation Area are the hardy 5-mile *Twin Valley Trail* and the sporty 2-mile *Millstone Trail* with its scenic rock outcroppings and two never-finished millstones. A half-mile *Logger's Trail* illuminates the history of lumbering in the area.

A third trailhead in White Clay is at the park office on Thompson Station Road. This rugged hill climb was the home site of David English, a lease holder of the William Penn family.

Bonus

In the southern part of White Clay, reached by the Twin Valley Trail, is the Arc Corner Monument marking one end of the 12-mile arc which forms the Pennsylvania-Delaware state line, unique in American political boundary-making. The circular divide dates to William Penn's directive of August 28, 1701, when Delaware was still a part of Pennsylvania, known as the Lower Three Counties. A little more than 1/2 mile to the west is another monument marking the tri-state junction of Delaware, Pennsylvania and Maryland.

The *Penndel Trail*, over three miles in length, connects the park and the preserve. It is a superb linear trail that picks up the east branch of the White Clay Creek, crosses the Middle Branch and continues along the main waterway. Flat for its entire length, it is, save for undergrowth near the Middle Branch, uniformly wide. There are also eight miles of bridle trails across the fields and on the opposite side of the stream in the preserve.

Trail Sense. The paths are blazed, the paths are named and there is an excellent color map. But some stretches share two or three trails so pay attention.

Dog Friendliness

All trails and most areas of the parks are open to dogs.

Traffic

The preserve is less visited than the state park. Many of the trails are open to bikes and horses as well as hikers.

Canine Swimming

The swift and shallow White Clay Creek is the purest around for drinking. Occasional pools will host some dog-paddling along the way. There is good swimming in the Millstone Pond in the Carpenter Recreation Area and in two farm ponds on the *David English Trail*.

Trail Time

More than an hour.

5

Scott Arboretum

The Park

The 300-acre Swarthmore campus is developed to be an arboretum, established in 1929 as a living memorial to Arthur Hoyt Scott, Class of 1895. The 3,000 different kinds of plants have been chosen as suggestions for the best trees, shrubs, perennials and annuals to use in home gardens in the Delaware Valley.

The Walks

Several area colleges welcome responsible dog owners - Swarthmore's Scott Arboretum serves the best canine hiking. The plant collections are integrated with the stone buildings of the college that dates to 1864. Leaving the cultivated plantings of the campus, a variety of hillside trails lead through the 200-acre Crum Woods down to Crum Creek.

Trail Sense: Brochures and mapboards lead you around these delightful walks.

Dog Friendliness

Dogs are not only welcomed at Swarthmore, but there are water bowls chained to some of the drinking fountains. In the Crum Woods your dog need only be under voice control, not leashed.

Delaware County

Distance from Philadelphia
- 15 miles
Phone Number
- (610) 328-8025
Website
- www.scottarboretum.org
Admission Fee
- None
Directions
- The Scott Arboretum is in Swarthmore on Chester Road (Route 320) between I-95 and Baltimore Pike. Parking for the arboretum is just inside the entrance on College Road, on the left.

Traffic

A campus walk when school is not in session is a dog-walking pleasure. There will be plenty of streets to cross here, however.

Canine Swimming

Crum Creek is deep enough in many places to permit limited canine swimming.

Trail Time

Less than an hour.

6

Woodlawn Trustees Property

The Park

From 1850 until 1910, feldspar, used in porcelain dishes and false teeth, was mined here in the Woodlawn Quarry. You can still see the remains of these spar pits, with their scatterings of mica and other minerals. In 1910, as his campaign to preserve the Brandywine Valley intensified, William Poole Bancroft bought hundreds of pristine acres in the lush floodplain and rolling woodlands where the Brandywine Creek makes three wide, gentle turns. Bancroft formed the Woodlawn Company to manage these lands, harboring some of the oldest trees in Delaware. Today, more than 2,000 acres are open to the public for hiking and riding.

The Walks

Miles of informal trails can be combined to create any kind of day out with your dog. Athletic dogs will enjoy romping across the grassy hills above the Brandywine Creek. Walking back and forth on the *Fire Trail* along the water provides an easy 45-minute walk.

New Castle County

Distance from Philadelphia
- 26 miles
Phone Number
- None
Website
- None
Admission Fee
- None
Directions
- There are no highway signs to direct you here and the parking lots are marked only with rules posters. The main parking lot is opposite Peters Rock along the Brandywine Creek on Creek Road. Other gravel parking lots can be found on Ramsey Road, Beaver Valley Road and opposite Woodlawn Road on Thompson's Bridge Road (Route 92). All are just off Route 202, making the first right after entering Delaware. Trail access can also be made from a parking lot in the hotel complex on Route 202.

The trails can be jumping off points for hikes of several hours duration. Following the white blazes of the Wilmington Trail Club along the Brandywine Creek you can cross Smith Bridge Road and follow the trail up to Chadds Ford. This involves a short walk, with little shoulder, on Creek Road and the trail is too rough and narrow to keep a dog leashed comfortably. You can also cross Beaver Valley Road into Pennsylvania and loop around the fast-flowing Beaver Run. The trail is hilly and requires some careful creek crossings but is very scenic. Finally you can cross Thompson's Bridge Road and walk into the Brandywine Creek State Park.

Trail Sense: The trails are unmarked, no map is available but orientating yourself to the river and roads should prevent any confusion.

Dog Friendliness

There are no prohibitions against dogs on the Woodlawn Trustees property.

Traffic

In recent years the Woodlawn Trustees property has become a favorite track for mountain bikers. There is also the good chance of encountering horses on the trail.

Canine Swimming

The shallow Brandywine Creek is an excellent swimming creek for dogs with many easy access points from the trail.

Trail Time

More than an hour.

7

Green Lane Park

The Park

Public recreation here dates to 1939 with the founding of Upper Perkiomen Valley Park. Upon its wedding to Green Lane Reservoir Park, the largest single open space purchase-easement in Montgomery County history, Green Lane Park, was created. The focal point of the 3100-acre park is the Green Lane Reservoir, home to more than a dozen species of freshwater fish.

The Walks

Four of the five trails here are open to dogs (four-legged friends are not welcome on the *Hemlock Point Trail*). The *Red Trail*, designed as an equestrian trail but not chewed up like so many other such surfaces, winds through open fields and stands of trees for 10 miles, although the entire length can be aborted in several places. The premier trail at Green Lane Park is the heavily wooded *Blue Trail* on the western edge of the reservoir where you pick your way across steep ravines and narrow ridges for 6 miles. Watch for passages over loose rocks. The full loop can be cut off at the Turn Around but you'll miss the extravagant rock carvings of falling water at work. At the Hill Road Office, and overlapping the Blue Trail, is the *Whitetail Trail*,

Montgomery County

Distance from Philadelphia
 - 39 miles
Phone Number
 - (215) 234-8684
Website
 - www.montcopa.org/parks/greenlane.htm
Admission Fee
 - None
Directions
 - Green Lane Park is in northwestern Montgomery County. Heading north on Route 29 there are several approaches to the trails. For the Orange Trail, make a left on Snyder Road, drive through the recreation area to the parking lot on Deep Creek Road. For the Blue Trail, make a left on Park Road and a right on Hill Road to the trailhead on the left. The Red Trail is just off Route 29 on Knight Road.

a self-guided nature walk.

There are hilly climbs throughout Green Lane Park; the gentlest terrain is found on the Red Trail.

Trail Sense: A good trail map is available - and do not let go of it. The trails are blazed, but not always energetically. The Red Trail uses ribbons which are sometimes tied to fallen posts. Among the things NOT to try at Green Lane: following the *Orange Trail* from the parking lot as indicated on the map (it is not marked) and trying the Red Trail clockwise (there is a reason the map uses directional arrows).

Dog Friendliness

There is plenty of room to hike with the dog at Green Lane without missing the forbidden Hemlock Point Trail.

Traffic

Most of the people who use the recreational areas of this popular park are not even aware of some of the trails in the far reaches of Green Lane. Especially on the Red Trail you can count on blocking out long stretches of trail time without seeing a soul.

Canine Swimming

There is excellent access to the reservoir from the Blue Trail; less so on the Red Trail.

Trail Time

More than an hour.

"Dogs' lives are too short. Their only fault, really."
-Agnes Sligh Turnbull

8

Ridley Creek State Park

The Park

Settlement in this area dates back to the 1600s when villages grew around the mills sprinkled along the creeks and streams. Much of the park's 2,606 acres were consolidated in the Jefford family - their *Hunting Hill* mansion, built in 1914 around a 1789 stone farmhouse, now serves as the park office. The Commonwealth of Pennsylvania purchased the property in the 1960s - including 35 historic residences - and the park was dedicated in 1972.

Delaware County

Distance from Philadelphia
 - 14 miles
Phone Number
 - (610) 892-3900
Website
 - www.dcnr.state.pa.us/
   stateparks/parks/r-crek.htm
Admission Fee
 - None
Directions
 - Ridley Creek can be accessed from Route 3, 2.5 miles west of Newtown Square, past the Colonial Pennsylvania Plantation. The park may also be entered from Gradyville Road - east from Route 352 or west from Route 252.

The Walks

Ridley Creek features 12 miles of hiking on four main trails. The *White Trail* visits most of the areas of the park and the others intersect this lengthy loop at many points. A 5-mile multi-use loop is shared with bicyclists and joggers. Also, an unmarked trailhead just east of Ridley Creek on Gradyville Road offers one of the longest creekside walks in Delaware County. In addition, a 4.7-mile equestrian trail makes two large loops in the isolated western section of the park.

These heavily wooded trails are narrow in many places and you and the dog will be prime targets for hitchhiking ticks. Most of the trails wind through rolling woodland and meadows. You'll be moving up and down often but only an occasional hardy climb is necessary.

Trail Sense: The trails are blazed and easy to follow, except through the parking areas - keep your eye on the pavement here. A trail map is available.

Dog Friendliness

Dogs are welcome on all the trails; along the multi-use trail are metal doggie water bowls chained to the benches.

Traffic

If you opt off the Multi-Use Trail you can go miles in Ridley Creek without seeing other hikers and dogs. Bikes are not allowed off the paved trails.

Canine Swimming

Ridley Creek, while extremely scenic, is a relatively minor feature of hiking at Ridley Creek State Park. It is deep enough for swimming when the trail touches upon it. There are no ponds on the property.

Trail Time

More than an hour.

9

Fair Hill Natural Area

The Park

Located just across the Delaware state line, this is the Godzilla of area hiking. Traversing its 5,613 acres are over 75 miles of multi-use trails. Fair Hill was formerly owned by sportsman William du Pont, Jr. and was one of the largest private land holdings on the East Coast. The State of Maryland purchased the estate in 1975 to develop for public use.

The Walks

Trails through the fields are typically double-track (old dirt vehicle roads). Singletrack trails dominate in the forested areas. Many roll through golden hayfields as befits Fair Hill's stature as a leading equine training center. The stiffest climbs are in the vicinity of the Big Elk Creek but most of the trails are like walking a steeplechase course.

The Big Elk Creek surges through the property and is spanned by many trail bridges, including one of Maryland's six remaining covered bridges. The Big Elk Creek Covered Bridge was built in 1860 at a cost of $1,165. When it was reconstructed in 1992 after sustaining extensive damage from heavy trucks, the tab was $152,000. Fair Hill is also a good place to walk past house ruins.

Cecil County

Distance from Philadelphia
- 47 miles

Phone Number
- (410) 398-1246

Website
- www.dnr.state.md.us/publiclands/central/fairhill.html

Admission Fee
- $2.00 parking fee

Directions
- Fair Hill is just west of Newark. Take Route 273 across the Maryland-Delaware State line until the first four-way intesection, Appleton Road, about 1.2 miles. There is parking down either side of Appleton Road. The Park Office is on Route 273, behind the grandstands for the Fair Hill Race Track.

Trail Sense: The trails are not marked and there are times you can feel like a real explorer when you leave the doubletrack trails. Unless you enjoy that feeling all day, a trail map from the office is mandatory. Be aware - there are more dead ends here than in an English maze garden.

Dog Friendliness

Dogs are allowed on the trails at Fair Hill.

Traffic

There is competition on the trails from mountain bikers and horses but fellow trail users are like bottles in the ocean in this vast property.

Canine Swimming

The Big Elk Creek runs swift and shallow through the park - deep enough for trout to swim but not for dogs.

Trail Time

More than an hour.

"The greatest pleasure of a dog is that you may make a fool of yourself with him, and not only will he not scold you, but will make a fool of himself too."

- Samuel Butler

10

Wharton State Forest

The Park

Wharton State Forest lies at the heart of New Jersey's mysterious Pine Barrens, a tapestry of impenetrable scrub pine, swamps and bogs. Today known for its cranberry and blueberry production, the area's bog ore once supported a booming iron industry which supplied much of the weaponry for the American Revolution. Many of the indecipherable sand roads through the Pine Barrens date to that time. When the foundries followed the discovery of America's massive upper midwestern iron ranges in the mid-1800s, the area's economy became so depressed that Philadelphia financier Joseph Wharton was able to acquire over 100,000 acres of land here. That land now makes up the state forest - the largest single tract of land in the New Jersey state park system.

Burlington County

Distance from Philadelphia
- 45 miles
Phone Number
- (609) 561-0024
Website
- www.state.nj.us/dep/
 forestry/parks/wharton.htm
Admission Fee
- Parking fee charged weekends in season at Batsto
Directions
- Wharton State Forest has two offices: at Batsto Village on Route 542, eight miles east of Hammonton, and at Atsion Recreation Area on Route 206, eight miles north of Hammonton.

The Walks

The main pathway is the *Batona Trail*, a 49-mile pink-blazed wilderness trail that begins at Ongs Hat in the north and ends at Lake Absegami in Bass River State Forest to the south. There are no loops so you must choose how far along the trail you and the dog want to go, then turn around and head back. Wild blueberries and huckleberries can be gathered by the bagful in sesaon. The hard-packed sand *Batona Trail*, that sports

44

some gentle undulations to break up a mostly flat walk, is a joy under paw and boot.

For those who feel cramped by the rigidness of a narrow 49-mile trail there are more than 500 miles of unpaved sand roads in Wharton State Forest. There is also a self-guided one-mile nature walk around the lake at Batsto Village, a restored 1800s village which was at the heart of the Pine Barrens economic life.

Trail Sense: The trail is well-marked and an excellent five-section trail map with distances is available.

Dog Friendliness

Dogs are welcome in the Wharton State Forest.

Traffic

Horseback riding and mountain bikes are not permitted on the Batona Trail.

Canine Swimming

An aquifer inside the Pine Barren's deep sand beds holds 17 trillion gallons of pure glacial water. The shallow aquifer often percolates to the surface in the form of bogs, marshes and swamps. The Batsto River is stained the color of tea by cedar sap, adding to the region's mystique. It makes an excellent canine swimming pool.

Trail Time

More than an hour.

11

Brandywine Creek State Park

The Park

Once a duPont family dairy farm, this spectacular swath of land became a State Park in 1965. Delaware's first two nature preserves are located here: Tulip Tree Woods, behind the park office, and Freshwater Marsh, at the edge of Brandywine Creek. The stone walls that criss-cross the 850-acre park are the legacy of skilled Italian masons who crafted the barriers from locally quarried Brandywine granite - the original "Wilmington Blue Rocks."

The Walks

There are eight blazed trails totalling 14 miles on both

New Castle County

Distance from Philadelphia
 - 27 miles
Phone Number
 - (302) 577-3534
Website
 - www.destateparks.com/bcsp/bcsp.htm
Admission Fee
 - Fee charge daily from Memorial Day-Labor Day and weekends in May, September and October
Directions
 - The main entrance is on Adams Dam Road, between Thompson's Bridge Road (Route 92) and Rockland Road. Other parking areas are at Thompson's Bridge and off Rockland Road, opposite Rockland Mills.

sides of the Brandywine Creek. All are short, all are woodsy and if you can't reach out and touch the water you are moving up or down a hill. The *Hidden Pond Trail* and the *Indian Springs Trail* each travel along the water, immerse you in the steep valley terrain and traverse the Tulip Tree Woods, where majestic tulip poplar have grown for nearly two centuries.

The star walk at Thompson's Bridge is the rugged *Rocky Run Trail*, winding around the closest thing to a mountain stream in Delaware. On this trail you'll discover fragrant stands of hemlock nestled among hardwood neighbors. Nearby, the *Multi-Use Trail* tags Brandywine Creek for the better part of two miles.

Trail Sense: All the paths are blazed and there is an excellent color map available.

Dog Friendliness

Dogs are welcome on all trails.

Traffic

Brandywine Creek State Park is a heavily used park; the trails at Thompson's Bridge are less crowded than the main park. Bikes are restricted to the Multi-Use Trail.

Canine Swimming

The Brandywine Creek is one of the best places in Delaware to take your dog for a swim. There is plenty of access to the water from the low banks.

Trail Time

More than an hour.

12

Ralph Stover /
Tohickon Valley Park

The Park

Ralph Stover State Park takes its name from the operator of a water-powered grain mill on the Tohickon Valley Creek in the late 1700s. Traces of the historic mill can still be seen above the dam. The Stover descendents donated the property to Pennsylvania in 1931 and recreational facilities in the 45-acre park were constructed during the 1930s by the Works Project Administration The High Rocks area was donated by Bucks County author James Michener.

Bucks County

Distance from Philadelphia
 - 31 miles
Phone Number
 - (610) 982-5560
Website
 - www.dcnr.state.pa.us/
 stateparks/ralph.htm
Admission Fee
 - None
Directions
 - Ralph Stover State Park is
two miles north of Point
Pleasant on State Park Road
and Stump Road. Tohickon
Valley Park is two miles down
Cafferty Road off Route 32.

The Walks

The *Red Dot Trail* sweeps in a wide arc for 5.5 miles connecting the two parks. Upon reaching the top of the High Rocks it is easy to feel like you have been parachuted into the heart of the Applachian mountains. Two hundred feet below you stretches a hillside tapestry of trees collared by a horsehoe turn in the Tohickon Creek. There is no similar view in the Delaware Valley. The trail itself rolls up and down across several ravine-slashing creeks. The dirt path is wide and easy on the paws, save for a steady diet of hopping on and across exposed tree roots.

Three short walking trails course through Ralph Stover State Park and additional trails are maintained in Tohickon Valley Park across the creek for extended canine hiking.

Trail Sense: The "Red Dot" trail is well-blazed and a trail map is available.

Dog Friendliness
Dogs are welcome in the park.

Traffic
The "Red Dot" trail is popular with mountain bikers; foot traffic thins considerably away from the High Rocks vista.

Canine Swimming
The fast-flowing waters of the Tohickon can be treacherous when the water is high.

Trail Time
More than an hour.

13

Washington Crossing State Park

The Park

These sleepy, tree-lined banks along the Delaware River became immortalized in American mythology on the icy night of December 25, 1776 when General George Washington led a demoralized Continental Army across the river to score a surprise victory over partying Hessian troops in Trenton. Land was eventually preserved on both the New Jersey and Pennsylvania sides of the river to commemorate one of the turning points in the battle for independence.

Mercer County

Distance from Philadelphia
- 34 miles
Phone Number
- (609) 737-0623
Website
- www.state.nj.us/dep/
  forestry/parks/washcros.htm
Admission Fee
- None
Directions
- From Interstate-95, take Route 29 north. Parking is available along the Delaware River just past Route 546.

The Walks

There are dog-walking opportunities on both sides of the Delaware; the more historic explorations can be found on the Pennsylvania side, the more natural trails in New Jersey. Quiet paths meander through an historic village at the scene of the American disembarkment in Washington's Crossing Historic Park.

On the New Jersey side, the terrain instantly becomes rolling and wooded beyond the Johnson Ferry House where the troops landed in what is now Washington Crossing State Park. The many miles of trails are carved through a mixed hardwood and spruce forest, often times plunging into and out of wide ravines.

Washington Crossing State Park can also be used as a jumping off point for hikes up and down the towpath along the 70-mile Delaware and Raritan Canal.

Trail Sense: The trails are not blazed and maps are not available.

Dog Friendliness

Dogs can enjoy the New Jersey trails and look at the outside of buildings in Washington Crossing Historic Park's McConkey's Ferry Section. Dogs are not allowed in Bowman's Hill Wildflower Preserve upstream in the Thompson's Mill Section.

Traffic

The towpath is popular with joggers and bicyclists but the crowds thin out on the hills of the state park.

Canine Swimming

There is no good access to the Delaware River at this point.

Trail Time

More than an hour.

"The best thing about a man is his dog."
-French Proverb

14

Middle Run Valley
Natural Area

The Park

The White Clay Creek drains some 70,000 acres and 100 square miles in Pennsylvania and Delaware. In Delaware, where Middle Run is one of its three main tributaries, it seems that much of that watershed is choked by suburban sprawl. Beginning in 1975, local civic and environmental groups began piecemeal acquisition of pristine woodlands that has resulted in an 850-acre oasis in the center of housing subdivisions, shopping centers and busy roadways.

New Castle County

Distance from Philadelphia
- 40 miles
Phone Number
- None
Website
- None
Admission Fee
- None
Directions
- Middle Run is northeast of Newark. From Kirkwood Highway (Route 2) follow Possum Park Road 1.7 miles to Possum Hollow Road on the right. Take a left at the entrance to the park after about 1/2 mile.

The Walks

Middle Run features splendid canine hiking on five well-maintained loop trails that cover 14 miles and an additional five short spurs that lead to surrounding communites. All offer interesting - and sometimes challenging - changes in terrain. There is almost 200 feet of elevation change at Middle Run. The purple-blazed *Lenape Trail* visits most of the property in its run of almost 7 miles, one of the longest loop trails in Delaware. The best choice for dog walkers only wanting to sample Middle Run's sylvan charms is the pedestrian-only 2.15-mile *Possum Hollow Trail*. All the natural dirt and grass trails bound up and down hills but the *Snow Geese Trail*, marked in orange on the east side of the park, is an especially steep, heart-pumping loop for canine and human.

Trail Sense: The trails are not continually blazed but markers direct the way at trail junctions. Still, don't be surprised if you find yourself walking unintentionally down a trail you didn't start on. New Castle County publishes a superb trail map and brochure but it is available only in county offices, not at the park. The map board at the Possum Hollow Road parking lot is the best in the tri-state area to help guide you.

Dog Friendliness

Dogs are welcome on all trails.

Traffic

Even though the parking lot has room for only 24 cars, it seems frivilously large most of the time. No one stumbles upon Middle Run. There are no directional signs announcing its existence from any of the major roads enclosing this natural area. Expect little company on these trails although there is an active community of mountain bikers that ride here.

Canine Swimming

There are no ponds on the property and the Middle Run and its branches are too shallow for swimming. There is enough water, however, for splashing on a hot day.

Trail Time

More than an hour.

15

Fort Mott State Park

The Park

Fort Mott was envisioned as part of a three-fort defense of Philadelphia that dangled across the Delaware River. Following the Civil War, work began on 11 gun emplacements but only two were completed when the fort was abandoned in 1876. In preparation for the Spanish-American War in 1896, Fort Mott, named to honor Major General Gershom Mott, a native of Bordentown, was completed and outfitted with three 10-inch and three 12-inch guns.

Salem County

Distance from Philadelphia
- 36 miles
Phone Number
- (609) 935-3218
Website
- www.state.nj.us/dep/
forestry/parks/fortmot.htm
Admission Fee
- None
Directions
- From Exit 1 of Interstate 295, take Route 49 East to Fort Mott Road. Turn right onto Fort Mott Road and travel 3 miles. Park is located on right.

The fort remained active until 1943, although during its last two decades the guns were dismantled and shipped elsewhere. In 1947 the State of New Jersey purchased Fort Mott as an historic site and opened the state park on June 24, 1951.

The Walks

Fort Mott features a walking tour through the 19th century defensive position that enables your dog to ramble through the gun batteries and ammunition magazines and to clamber on top of the massive protective parapet. This concrete wall was built of concrete poured 35 feet thick with an additional 60 feet of earth piled in front. Landscaping made the fort look like a big hill from the Delaware River.

In additon to this unique dog walk there is a groomed trail that winds through twelve-foot high swamp grasses to Finn's

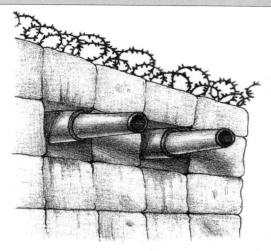

Point National Cemetery, the final resting place for 2,436 Confederate soldiers who perished in a Civil War prisoner of war camp at Fort Delaware on the Delaware River.

Trail Sense: A map of the walking tour is available.

Dog Friendliness

Dogs are permitted in the park.

Traffic

Not many people make their way to this remote outpost on the banks of the Delaware River.

Canine Swimming

Fort Mott State Park is the closest thing to an ocean swimming experience in the Delaware Valley. Below the ferry pier is a sand beach with enough wave action to convince your dog he's chasing that stick into the Atlantic.

Trail Time

Less than an hour.

16

Tyler State Park

The Park

The rolling lands along the Neshaminy Creek here have supported a vibrant farming community for over 300 years. Some of the stone dwellings peppered around the property date to the early 1700s. Funding from Pennsylvania conservation programs resulted in the opening of Tyler State Park in 1974. Today, more than 400 of the park's 1,711 acres are still under cultivation.

The Walks

Neshaminy Creek bisects Tyler State Park into two distinctly different halves. The eastern side is distinguished by a tightly bunched network of gravel hiking paths connecting the popular recreational areas located in this section of the park. The trails are shady and hilly.

Bucks County

Distance from Philadelphia
- 31 miles
Phone Number
- (215) 968-2021
Website
- www.dcnr.state.pa.us/
  stateparks/tyler.htm
Admission Fee
- None
Directions
- Tyler State Park is in Newtown, reached via the Pennsylvania Turnpike. From Exit 27 follow Route 332 east to the park entrance at the intersection of Swamp Road and the four-lane bypass. From Exit 28 take Route 1 North to I-95 North to Exit 30 for Newtown-Yardley and follow the bypass west.

Across the creek, the trails stretch out for longer walks. There are more than ten miles of paved multi-purpose bicycle trails and almost as many miles of dirt-and-grass bridle paths. The trail system, one of the most elaborate in greater Philadelphia, can be customized into an endless array of short or long hikes. The terrain remains hilly, especially on the steep, self-guiding nature trail that loops its way around Parker Run as it feeds into Neshaminy Creek.

Trail Sense: In the western section of Tyler State Park the trails are named at their junctions and a detailed park map is available.

Dog Friendliness

Dogs are welcome on all trails in the park.

Traffic

Tyler is a busy place, pulsing with scores of walkers, cyclists and equestrians. The further you push from the heart of the park, the lighter the traffic becomes. There are parking lots near the outer perimeter of the park that permit access to the more remote trails.

Canine Swimming

The Neshaminy Creek is an excellent venue for canine aquatics with many access points from the trail above the dam.

Trail Time

More than an hour.

"My dog can bark like a Congressman, fetch like an aide, beg like a press secretary and play dead like a receptionist."
-Gerald Solomon

17

Schuylkill Canal Park

The Park

Pennsylvania's first canal system was cobbled together in 1815 using 120 locks to stretch 108 miles from the coal fields of Schuylkill County to Philadelphia. Railroads began chewing away at canal business in the 1860s and the last coal barges floated down the Schuylkill River in the 1920s. Today, the only sections of the canal in existence are at Manayunk and Lock 60, built by area name donor Thomas Oakes, at the Schuylkill Canal Park. In 1985 the Schuylkill Canal Association formed to keep the canal flowing and maintain the lock and towpath. In 1988, the area was added to the National Register of Historic Places.

Montgomery County

Distance from Philadelphia
 - 22 miles
Phone Number
 - None
Website
 - None
Admission Fee
 - None
Directions
 - The Schuylkill Canal Park is in Mont Clare, on Route 29 across the Schuylkill River from Phoenixville. Crossing the river on Bridge Street, make a left at the end of the bridge onto the entrance road for the upstream parking area. To reach the downstream parking lot, make the right at the light onto Port Providence Road and follow it through town and past the Container Corporation of America.

Quality of Hikes

You can either enjoy the flattest walk in Montgomery County here or the steepest. The peaceful canal towpath covers 2 1/2 miles from the Lock House, built in 1836, to the eastern end of Port Providence. Across the canal are houses and town buildings looking much as they did throughout the canal era.

Upstream from Lock 60 are the *Ravine Trail*, with three ascents to the 100-foot high rock bluffs overlooking the Schuylkill

River, and the *Valley View Trail,* which deadends - for dog-walking - at the Upper Schuylkill Valley Park. No dogs are allowed in that park. There is also an 8-station self-guided nature walk from the Lock House to Route 29.

Trail Sense.   There are no consistent trail markings here.

Dog Friendliness

This is one of the friendliest, most relaxed parks in the area.

Traffic

Very light; your primary worry being the entrance road which is only 1 1/2 cars wide.

Canine Swimming

Virtually every step of the way there is great access to either the Schuylkill River or the Schuylkill Canal.

Trail Time

More than an hour.

18

Parvin State Park

Park History

The first landowner of these diverse pinelands was John Estaugh, husband of Elizabeth Haddon, who lived in present-day Haddonfield. Estaugh was granted 2,928 acres on March 31, 1742, by the Proprietors of West Jersey. Development began in 1796 when Lemuel Parvin purchased the property with the intention of operating a sawmill. He created Parvin Lake by constructing an earthen dam across Muddy Run on its journey to the Maurice River.

Salem County

Distance from Philadelphia
- 32 miles
Phone Number
- (609) 358-8616
Website
- www.state.nj.us/dep/
  forestry/parks/parvin.htm
Admission Fee
- None
Directions
- Parvin State Park is six miles west of Vineland on Route 540, just east of the intersection with Route 553.

The State of New Jersey's stewardship began in 1930 with the acquisition of 918 acres of forest and the 108-acre lake. During the Depression the Civilian Conservation Corps established a camp at Parvin, building campgrounds and cabins and carving trails. In 1944, German prisoners of war from Fort Dix were housed in Parvin while working on local farms and food processing plants. The POWS were captured from German Field Marshall Erwin Rommell's marauding Afrika Corps.

Many of the facilities built by the Civilian Conservation Corps are still in use in the park today.

The Walks

A variety of loops and linear trails slice across Parvin State Park's 1,135 acres, about evenly divided between a recreational area and a natural area. The hiking is easier in the recreational area with its wide, packed-sand trails. The trails narrow in the oak-pine forests, cedar swamps and laurel thickets of the natural area. These scenic woodlands on the fringe of the Pine Barrens are home to 40 known types of trees, 61 different woody shrubs and 17 ferns and club mosses. All the walking on the nine named trails, totalling more than 15 miles, is flat.

Trail Sense: Only trailheads on the major trails are marked and trail blazes disappear in the natural area. Don't let go of the park map on long hikes.

Dog Friendliness

All trails are open to dogs but they are not permitted in the campgrounds and cabins and in the Parvin Grove beach area.

Traffic

This is not a heavily used park and away from the campgrounds and picnic groves isolation is virtually assured. Only a few trails are hiker-only, however.

Canine Swimming

There is excellent doggie paddling in the attractive Parvin Lake and there is abundant access to the water in smaller Thundergast Lake. Although access is limited, the swimming is also good in the deceptively-named Muddy Run.

Trail Time

More than an hour.

"If there are no dogs in Heaven,
then when I die I want to go where they went."
-Anonymous

19

Darlington Trail

Park History

The Darlington Trail was developed by Middletown Township, preserving space near the former Darlington Family Dairy Farm.

The Walks

Half of the yellow-blazed *Darlington Trail* hugs the heavily wooded Chester Creek valley and the other half traverses the meadows and fields of the former farmstead. The entire loop is approximately 2 3/4 miles long. The *Cornucopia Trail*, a shorter path blazed in orange, connects with the Darlington Trail and circumnavigates a residential area. The Darlington Trail also connects with the *Rocky Run Trail*, a scenic linear walk in open woodlands along the Chester Creek. The trails, for the most part, are wide and easy to negotiate.

To do the entire loop will require several steep climbs away from Chester Creek. You can also treat the trail as an out-and-back linear hike along the creekbed that creates an easy walk.

Trail Sense: The trails are well-marked; there is a detailed map posted on the board at the trailhead.

Dog Friendliness

Dogs are welcome to hike along here.

Delaware County

Distance from Philadelphia
- 19 miles
Phone Number
- (610) 469-4900
Website
- None
Admission Fee
- None
Directions
- Darlington Trail is in Middletown Township. A small parking lot for the Darlington Trail is located on Darlington Road, 1/2 mile from Route 1. The parking lot is marked by a trailhead sign.

Traffic

Despite being in the shadow of Route 1, the Darlington Trail is lightly used - the parking lot scarcely holds a half dozen vehicles.

Canine Swimming

At a 270-degree turn in the Chester Creek behind the parking lot, the banks are sandy, giving your dog the opportunity for a rare Delaware County beach experience. Rocky Run, which joins the Chester Creek on the trail is more for splashing.

Trail Time

More than an hour.

20

McKaig Nature Education Center

Park History

The Upper Merion Park and Historic Foundation was created in 1964 to preserve the area's rapidly diminishing open space. Small accruals of land gifts began accumulating and today the McKaig Nature Education Center pushes back the encroaching development with 89 wooded acres.

The Walks

A jewel among the region's small parks, McKaig features three wide and well-maintained trails that range in walking time from 15 minutes to 45 minutes. The *Cadet Trail* is a linear exploration running up the spine of the property. Two loop trails branch off the Cadet: the *Nancy Long Trail* and the short, but steep *Laurel Trail*. The loops are hillier than the Cadet Trail but the trails work around the hillside rather than straight up the slopes on these sporty walks.

Trail Sense: The Cadet Trail (white blazes) and the Nancy Long Trail (yellow blazes) are well-marked. The Laurel Trail is unmarked; look for the entrance under a fallen tree.

Montgomery County

Distance from Philadelphia
- 20 miles
Phone Number
- None
Website
- None
Admission Fee
- None
Directions
- In Upper Merion, McKaig Nature Education Center is bounded roughly by King of Prussia Road, Brower Road and Croton Road. Parking is available on Brower Road (one or two cars on the roadside) and at the Roberts School on Croton Road. From Route 202, take Warner Road south to the end. Make a left on Croton Road and the school is on the right.

Dog Friendliness

Dogs are welcome on the trails in the McKaig Nature Education Center.

Traffic

Expect your visit to be a solitary experience.

Canine Swimming

The Crow Creek is a tumbling, pleasing little brook but seldom deep enough for anything beyond doggie splashing.

Trail Time

Less than an hour.

"They are superior to human beings as companions. They do not quarrel or argue with you. They never talk about themselves but listen to you while you talk about yourself, and keep an appearance of being interested in the conversation."

-Jerome K. Jerome

21

Lebanon State Forest

The Park

It is hard to imagine this vast 32,000 acre forest was stripped, barren land a little more than a century ago. The Lebanon Glass Works, from which the forest takes its name, set up shop in 1851 and within 16 years had devoured every stick of timber for miles in every direction. With its supply of wood depleted the furnace was shut down and abandoned. The state began buying the land that ultimately

Burlington County

Distance from Philadelphia
- 38 miles
Phone Number
- (609) 08064
Website
- www.state.nj.us/dep/
forestry/parks/lebanon.htm
Admission Fee
- None
Directions
- The Lebanon State Forest is accessible by State Highway Routes 70 and 72.

became Lebanon State Forest in 1908 and once again the sandy soil is blanketed with stands of pine, oak, maple, gum and Atlantic white cedar.

The Walks

If you are not in the mood for hours and hours of flat, level walking where the view seldom changes, do not bring the dog to Lebanon State Forest. Ongs Hat, at the western tip of the park, is the northern terminus for the *Batona Trail* and about 9 miles of the 49-mile route slice across the lower edge of Lebanon. Another good walking choice is the *Cranberry Trail* which runs 5 miles to Pakin Pond. For the more adventurous canine hiker there are over 20 miles of wilderness trails and if your restless spirit is still not sated it is easy to get off the grid here: Lebanon State Forest features 400 miles of unpaved roads. The trails are almost uniformly soft and easy on the paw.

Trail Sense: If you spend any time at all in Lebanon State

Forest you will get lost. A park map marks major trails and roads and hold on tight for orientation. If it's hot make sure you have plenty of drinking water and insect repellent.

Dog Friendliness

Dogs are permitted on trails throughout the forest but are not allowed in campgrounds.

Traffic

If you are looking to lose yourself in nature, this is the place.

Canine Swimming

The terrain is pocked with small ponds and creeks that make for superb swimming holes.

Trail Time

More than an hour.

*"A door is what a dog is perpetually on the
wrong side of."*

-James Thurber

22

Neshaminy State Park

Park History

Neshaminy State Park takes its name from the confluence of Neshaminy Creek with the Delaware River. Although the water flows another 116 miles to the Atlantic Ocean, the river is still affected by the tides here. Indian tribes congregated here to build fishing weirs, small fences in the water that fish swim over at high tide and become trapped at low tide. Dunken Williams operated a ferry crossing of the Delaware River at this point in 1679 and

Bucks County

Distance from Philadelphia
- 12 miles
Phone Number
- (215) 639-4538
Website
- www.dcnr.state.pa.us/
  stateparks/parks/nesh.htm
Admission Fee
- None
Directions
- From the Route 132 (Street Road) Exit of I-95 go east to State Road. Go left and the park is at the intersection of Dunks Ferry Road, less than one mile away.

Dunks Ferry Road on the eastern boundary of the park has been used for more than 300 years. The land was deeded to the Commonwealth of Pennsylvania in 1956.

The Walks

Neshaminy State Park is the best park in the area to experience the Delaware River. There are four miles of formal hiking trails on the 330-acre property shaped like a fingernail poking into the river. The *River View Trail* traces the shoreline providing access to the tidal marsh and river and affording riveting views of the ship traffic in the Delaware and the Philadelphia skyline. The *River Trail Inner Loop* explores the interior of the park. The *River Walk* is a shaded dirt trail; the inner loop is more open and follows a gravel road. There is an ample grass shoulder that that will save paws. Also available is the *Logan Walk*, a paved, tree-lined path that was the original

drive to the former Robert Logan Home, whose *Sarobia* estate was the foundation for the park.

Trail Sense: The trails are not blazed but a park map is available.

Dog Friendliness

Dogs are welcome along all the trails here but not permitted near the swimming pools at the center of the park.

Traffic

This is a busy park and moments of solitude will be found in bits and pieces and not large chunks.

Canine Swimming

There is some of the best canine swimming in the area at Neshaminy State Park with about a quarter-mile of open access to the Delaware River.

Trail Time

More than an hour.

23

Wenonah Woods

Park History

Wenonah grew out of a resort community that was founded in 1872, carved from the surrounding Deptford area. It was later the location of a junior-high and high-school level military academy, until the late 1930s. Interconnected wooded trails loop around the southern half of the town from northwest to east.

The Walks

From the north, across from Wenonah Lake, the first trail is *Break Back Run*, winding along wooded stream valleys and ridges. Next is the *Clay Hill Trail* where the walking is level save for the namesake hill by a bend in the stream. The well-maintained *Glen Trail* connects the paths on both sides of the railroad. A brief side trail to Clinton Street leads to a tiny, stone fish pond, a quaint remnant of Wenonah's 19th century resort days. Continuing onto the *George Eldridge Trail*, the path features many streams and wooden bridges. Side trails lead to more hiking on the *Deptford/Sewell Trails* and the *Monongahela Brook Trail*, a half-mile loop that rolls along the south shore and drops to a flat creekside return trip. Some of the biggest trees in the Wenonah Woods can be found here. The last trail is *Covey's Lake Trail*, a 3/4-mile loop along the quiet tree-lined shore. The lake was once a center for leisurely recreation at the resort, sporting a boathouse and a teahouse. Watch for snakes in the rocks around the lake.

Gloucester County

Distance from Philadelphia
- 15 miles

Phone Number
- None

Website
- www.geocities.com/ woodsofwenonah/html

Admission Fee
- None

Directions
- The town of Wenonah is on Route 553. The trails are accessed from several points around town including Hayes Road at East Mantua Avenue; the west end of West Cedar Street; and the east end of Pine Street.

Trail Sense: The trails are not marked but wooden posts are prominently placed at trail junctions.

Dog Friendliness

Dogs are welcome along all the trails here.

Traffic

There are backyards every 15 minutes or so but not much competition on the trails.

Canine Swimming

At the northern terminus of *Break Back Run Trail,* across N. Jefferson Avenue is Davidson's Lake, a super canine swimming hole. Comey's Lake is algae-encrusted but there is access to clear water near the wooden dock.

Trail Time

More than an hour.

24

Heinz National Wildlife Refuge

Park History

There are more than 500 National Wildlife Refuges in the United States and only Philadelphia and San Francisco offer an urban environmental study. When the Swedes settled here in 1634, Tinicum Marsh measured over 5,700 acres. Three hundred years later the tidal marsh had been reduced to only 200 acres. The routing of I-95 in 1969 threatened to finish off the marsh but, in ironic fact, saved it. Congress authorized the purchase of 1,200 acres in 1972, establishing the Tinicum National Environmental Center and enabling the highway to roar through the area.

The Walks

You can cover about ten miles of trails here in two major loops. The more attractive of the two is around the Impoundment Marsh near the Visitor Contact Station. If you have a patient dog you can pause at the Observation Platform or one of the Observation Blinds and try to identify one of the 288 species of birds seen in the refuge.

The western loop, that begins in Delaware County, leads onto a dike in the middle of the marsh and along the Darby Creek. The trail on the dike is narrow to the point of being overgrown during the spring and summer.

Trail Sense: The trail is not marked nor blazed but there is
a map available. It is not detailed and expect to take a detour
or two near the Route 420 parking area. Also, when walking along
I-95, keep to the highway side of the chain link fence.

Dog Friendliness

Dogs are welcome along all the trails here.

Traffic

There is little competition for space on these trails.

Canine Swimming

The Darby Creek is accessible but the fish pulled from these
waters are contaminated so you may want to limit water time here.

Trail Time

More than an hour.

25

Carousel Park

Park History

Carousel Park is another legacy to recreation in Delaware from the duPont family, being a former family estate. Long the home of public riding stables, New Castle County has worked to make the park a mecca for hiking as well.

The Walks

Carousel is a suburban park given over to walking - no playgrounds or ballfields here. The main trail (*The Carousel Loop*) is a three-mile walk around the circumference of the park. Many short connecting trails dissect the park as well. All told their are 14 trails in the park winding through open fields, horse pastures, ponds, hardwoods (*Land of the Giants*) and pine trees (*Sherwood Forest*). Carousel Park is set in rolling hills; a healthy climb is required to reach Strawberry Field in the back of the park. The Carousel Loop is covered with paw-pleasing wood chips the entire way while the connecting trails are gravel roads, dirt and sometimes grass.

Trail Sense: The trails are all well-marked, color-coded and sport whimsical names. Locator map boards are also on site.

New Castle County

Distance from Philadelphia
 - 38 miles
Phone Number
 - None
Website
 - None
Admission Fee
 - None
Directions
 - The main parking lot for Carousel Park, halfway between Newark and Wilmington, is on Limestone Road (Route 7) between Milltown Road and New Linden Hill Road. Smaller parking lots are at the end of Old Linden Hill Road, off Limestone Road, and on Skyline Drive, off New Linden Hill Road.

Dog Friendliness

Carousel Park is one of the most popular places to bring dogs in northern Delaware.

Traffic

There is some horse traffic from the equestrian course and plenty of walkers, joggers and other dogs on the trails.

Canine Swimming

A trail encircles Enchanted Lake, an ideal spot for canine aquatics. Another smaller swimming hole is the less fashionable Moonlight Pond.

Trail Time

Less than an hour.

"Any man who does not like dogs and want them does not deserve to be in the White House."
-Calvin Coolidge

26

Taylor Arboretum

The Park

The ownership of this property dates to William Penn who sold a thousand-acre land grant to John Sharpless in 1682. Sharpless descendents operated grist and cotton mills here for nearly two centuries. Taylor Memorial Arboretum was established in 1931 by a Chester lawyer, Joshua C. Taylor, in the memory of his wife, Anne Rulon Gray.

The Walks

The many trails through these 30 acres along Ridley Creek are short, interconnecting segments about evenly divided between woods and meadow. There are many highlights here, including plant-covered rock outcroppings, a bald cypress pond, and a groundwater spring. There is some slope on the property down to the floodplain of the Ridley Creek but the walking is easy. The trail surfaces are soft dirt and grass and pine straw.

Trail Sense: The trails are not blazed but a detailed site map is available. There is also a map board at the parking lot.

Dog Friendliness

As of this writing, Taylor Arboretum is one of the few remaining tree parks in the area that still allows dogs.

Delaware County

Distance from Philadelphia
- 17 miles
Phone Number
- (610) 876-2649
Website
- None
Admission Fee
- None
Directions
- Taylor Memorial Arboretum is located north of Chester. From I-95 take Exit 6 and follow Route 320 North. Just past 22nd Street, make a left on Chestnut Parkway and continue to the Arboretum entrance, making a left on Ridley Drive.

Traffic

This is a quiet, lightly-visited oasis.

Canine Swimming

The water behind the Sharpless Dam in the West Woods is excellent for canine swimming. In the East Woods the Ridley Creek offers a small stone beach and fast-flowing shallows for a doggie whirlpool.

Trail Time

Less than an hour.

"No animal should ever jump up on the dining room furniture unless...he can hold his own in the conversation."

-Fran Liebowitz

27

Hibernia County Park

The Park

Property deeds in this area date to October 1, 1765. In the 1790s, Samuel Downing built the first iron forge at Hibernia, along the West Branch of the Brandywine Creek. Downing lost his forge in a sheriff's sale in 1808 and the property then passed rapidly through many owners until Charles Brooke purchased the enterprise in 1821. He expanded its holdings to 1,710 acres and by the Civil War, the Hibernia Iron Works was churning pig iron into bar iron from two forges, two heating furnaces and a rolling mill.

Chester County

Distance from Philadelphia
- 47 miles
Phone Number
- (610) 384-0290
Website
-None
Admission Fee
- None
Directions
- Hibernia Park is four miles north of Coatesville. From Route 30, take Route 82 North two miles to Cedar Knoll Road, turn left and travel 1.25 miles to the main entrance.

The forge went silent in the 1870s. In 1894, Colonel Franklin Swayne, a successful Philadelphia real estate lawyer, purchased the property and transformed *Hibernia* (the Roman name for Ireland) into a gentleman's country estate. In 1963 the old ironmaster's mansion and nearly 900 acres of surrounding grounds passed to Chester County for renovation as a park.

The Walks

Hibernia features 5 main trails, all wooded and none longer than 1.5 miles. Only the *Cedar Hollow Trail* loops so you will need to combine park roads and unmarked paths to avoid retracing steps in your walking day. A dirt trail along the Brandywine is one of the longest waterside walks in Chester County.

Most of the walking is easy; there are slight hills down to the Brandywine Creek and the *Rim Trail* across the water requires a good climb to reach the ridge. Mostly the trails are dirt; the *Lake Trail* is paved with crushed stone.

Trail Sense: The trailheads are marked but some of the trails are more energetically marked than others. Do not let go of the trail map if you attempt to find the Rim Trail.

Dog Friendliness

Dogs are welcome along all the trails here.

Traffic

Hibernia is a popular park with facilities for camping and picnicing but it is possible to get away from the crowds, especially across the Brandywine Creek on the Rim Trail.

Canine Swimming

Dogs can enjoy a dip in the Brandywine Creek, a fishing pond or in Chambers Lake, where there is limited access to a 90-acre water reservoir created in 1994 with the damming of Birch Run.

Trail Time

More than an hour.

28

Brandywine - Rockford Park

The Park

Brandywine Park, Delaware's first park, created in 1885 and partially designed by Frederick Law Olmsted, can stand beside any of America's downtown river walks for person and dog. Rockford Park dates to 1889, when there were still fears of visitors being harmed by explosions in the DuPont Company black powder yards below. William Poole Bancroft began his life-long efforts to preserve open space in the Brandywine Valley here, with a gift of 59 acres. Today the park comprises 104 acres.

New Castle County

Distance from Philadelphia
- 29 miles
Phone Number
- None
Website
- None
Admission Fee
- None
Directions
- The main parking lot for Brandywine Park is on the north banks of the river at the foot of Monkey Hill, off of 18th and Van Buren streets. The entry way to Rockford Park is at 19th Street and Tower Road.

The Walks

The 1.8 mile *Brandywine Nature Trail* connects Brandywine Village and Rockford Park. Through Brandywine Park it runs along the north shore of the Brandywine River for about a mile. Once across the Swinging Bridge, the trail veers away from the water and towards Rockford Park via Kentmere Parkway. Along the way you'll enjoy native and ornamental plantings in the Rose Garden, the Waterwalk Garden, the Four Seasons Garden and elsewhere.

In Rockford Park the main walk is the circular road through the park, that goes past the 115-foot Rockford Tower, built in 1901. The stone water tower and its Observatory (132 steps to to the top) were once a popular tourist destination. There are

narrow, informal trails in the woods that run in parallel
terraces around the steep hill, including one on an old rail bed.
You can sculpt a flat walk by circling the road up top or
introduce a hill into your walk by descending "Sledding Hill" to
the lower field.

Trail Sense: There are several map boards in the park.

Dog Friendliness

There are off-leash sections in both Brandywine Park and
Rockford Park. You cannot walk your dog through the Brandywine Zoo in the park.

Traffic

This is the place to go to be with other dogs, not for solitary
dog-walking. Each evening in Rockford Park there is a Doggie
Social Hour on Sledding Hill. Dogs and owners gather to romp
and run one another ragged. The dogs that is.

Canine Swimming

Dogs can enjoy a dip in the Brandywine River and in the
mill race cut on the south side. In 1954, the Brandywine Canoe
Slalom, America's first ever slalom race for kayaks, ran in
these waters south of the Washington Street bridge. Two decades
later water kayaking would become a popular Olympic sport.

Trail Time

Less than an hour.

29

Nottingham County Park

The Park

Although this area had already been settled for nearly two centuries, it was not until 1828 that serpentinite was dicovered in what is now Nottingham Park. By 1880 the Wood Mine dug to extract the mineral was 800 feet deep and the largest in the world. Chrome, asbestos and quartz were also mined here. The oldest of Chester County's parks, Nottingham was dedicated in 1963.

The Walks

There are 8 trails in Nottingham Park, which can all be covered in a day's hiking. Most of the trails criss-cross and do not loop, often just running out at the boundaries of the 600-acre park. Look for the "Mystery Hole," an abandoned mine now filled with water. The dirt trails are generally wide through the rolling hills across the park. These hills can be formidable at times.

Trail Sense: The trails are blazed and named but study the available maps closely so you don't follow a trail to a dead-end at the back of the park without creating a loop. You will often be confronted with signposts at trail junctions. Choose wisely.

Dog Friendliness

Dogs are welcome along all the trails here.

Traffic

Tucked away in a remote corner of Chester County, the park does not get much visitation on the trails.

Canine Swimming

McPherson Lake and Little Pond are open-field swimming holes for a doggie dip.

Trail Time

More than an hour.

30

Norristown Farm Park

The Park

The area that is today Norristown Farm Park was part of a 7000-acre tract of land belonging to William Penn, known as "William-stadt." The ownership of the Norris family dates to October 10, 1704 when Penn's son sold the land to Isaac Norris and William Trent for the hefty sum of 850 pounds. On November 11, 1717, Trent sold his share of the manor to Norris.

After many subsequent lords, in 1876 the Pennsylvania legislature authorized the purchase of the manor for the Norristown State Hospital. The hospital eventually spread across 981 acres, 831 of which became a farm supplying not only food but a supposed conduit to patient recovery. Farm operations became too costly and ceased in 1975 and the farm fell into disrepair. In 1992, Montgomery County leased 690 acres to create the county's second largest park.

Montgomery County

Distance from Philadelphia
- 19 miles
Phone Number
- (610) 270-0215
Website
- www.dcnr.state.pa.us/ stateparks/norris.htm
Admission Fee
- None
Directions
- Norristown Farm Park is in northwestern Norristown. The main entrance is off Germantown Pike on Upper Farm Road (the first house on the right along the entrance road is Shannon Mansion, built in 1764 and the oldest building on the property). There is also parking on Whitehall Road.

The Walks

There are wide, multi-use trails totalling more than five miles at Norristown Farm Park. The trails roughly combine to form adjacent loops in a figure-eight pattern, passing through natural areas and cultivated fields of the revitalized farm where corn, soybeans and winter grains grow. The walking is easy across these rolling hills but there are long periods without shade for the heat-sensitive dog. All the trails are paved in macadam.

Trail Sense: A detailed trail map is available at the Milk House Visitor Center and is posted on boards in the parking lot.

Dog Friendliness

Dogs are welcome along all the trails in Norristown Farm Park.

Traffic

The paved trails are popular with cyclists, roller skaters and joggers. Your dog will need to be kept on a tight rein most of the time here.

Canine Swimming

Two branches of the Stony Creek knife through the property before joining at the baseball field into one stream. Although it reaches a swimming-friendly depth of four feet in places, the water is only accessed by the trail a few times.

Trail Time

More than an hour.

85

31

Oakbourne Park

The Park

John Hulme built the first granite shelter on this land, selecting the highest area on the property for his homesite. In 1882 a wealthy Philadelphia lawyer named James Smith purchased 143 acres of land on the west side of South Concord Road, including the old Hulme house. Smith renamed it *Oakbourne* and set more than 150 skilled craftsmen to work refurbishing his new summer home. Oakbourne was soon the centerpiece of a 27-acre estate with fountains, miniature lakes and rustic bridges. Smith even had its own private railroad station and post office.

Oakbourne was willed out of the Smith family to the Philadelphia Protestant Episcopal City Mission in 1896 for the operation of a convalescent home for women over 21 years of age. The next 70 years saw thousands of female "guests" treated here before the costly operation overwhelmed its directors. Westtown Township saved Oakbourne from developers in 1974, eventually creating a 90-acre park.

Chester County

Distance from Philadelphia
 - 36 miles
Phone Number
 - None
Website
 - None
Admission Fee
 - None
Directions
 - Oakbourne Park is in Westtown Township. Coming south on Route 202, make a left on Matlack Street, which runs into Oakbourne Road and South Concord Road. Make a right into the driveway and proceed past the mansion to the parking lot. Coming north on Route 202, make a right on Route 926 (Street Road) and a left on Concord Road. The park is on the left.

The Walks

Three connecting trails (*Creek, Nature* and *Park*) form a loop of nearly three miles to visit all areas of the park on both sides of Concord Road. The trails are all wooded, including native specimens and the remains of the Smiths' exotic plantings around the mansion. There is an interesting mix of terrain and sights on the remains of the country estate now engulfed by residential development. There are some dips and rolls in some of the wooded areas, including one good climb on the Creek Trail.

Trail Sense: The trails are haphazardly marked in places (the blazes are the smallest in Chester County) and can be hard to follow, especially picking the trail up across Concord Road. A mapboard is available near the parking lot.

Dog Friendliness

Dogs are welcome along all the trails here.

Traffic

The lightly tapped trails at Oakbourne are shoehorned into a tight geographic area that doesn't afford much isolation.

Canine Swimming

Part of the trail hopscotches past Chester Creek and one of Smith's miniature lakes, encircled by reeds, is a pleasant canine swimming stop.

Trail Time

Less than an hour.

32

Pennypack Preserve

The Park

The privately owned Pennypack Ecological Restoration Trust has been assembling a natural area preserve since 1970. Using land purchases, donations and conservation easements, the preserve has grown to 683 acres.

The Walks

There are 7 miles of trails here; dogs are allowed only in the Wilderness Area. Three connecting trails, each with its own personality, create a linear trail along the Pennypack Creek for about 2 1/2 miles. The longest, the *Deep Creek Road Trail*, is a country lane walk with plenty of access to the meandering stream. The middle leg, the *Pennypack Creek Trail*, hugs a hillside and is characterized by tall trees, especially conifers.

Montgomery County

Distance from Philadelphia
- 17 miles
Phone Number
- (215) 657-0830
Website
- www.liberty.net.org/pert/mission.htm
Admission Fee
- None
Directions
- The Pennypack Preserve is on the western edge of Bryn Athyn; the trailhead for the wilderness trails is at the corner of Terwood Road and Creek Road. From the intersection of Huntingdon Pike (Route 232) and Old Welsh Road (Route 63), go west on Old Welsh Road and make the first right across the bridge onto Terwood Road. Creek Road is one mile on the right. The trails can also be accessed from Mason's Mill Park on Mason's Mill Road.

The Pennypack Parkway is an old gravel access road, draped in a shaded canopy of trees. The walking here is mostly level with imperceptible ups and downs along the way.

Trail Sense: There are signposts and a trail map is available at the trailhead. Do not take any of the spur trails as they lead into the Environmental Management Center where dogs are not allowed.

Dog Friendliness

Although dogs are confined to the ribbon of trail along the Pennypack Creek, it is best remembered that most private nature preserves don't allow them at all.

Traffic

A long linear trail that requires a hiker's commitment, there is not as much traffic as the quality of the walk might otherwise inspire. There is some bicycle traffic to dodge.

Canine Swimming

The Pennypack Creek is seldom more than two feet deep, save for the base of Huntingdon Road where there are deep pools for doggie paddling.

Trail Time

More than an hour.

"And sometimes when you'd get up in the middle of the night you'd hear the reassuring thump, thump of her tail on the floor, letting you know that she was there and thinking of you."
-William Cole

33

Welkinweir

The Park

Welkinweir ("where sky meets water") was a foundering farm during the Depression when the property was purchased by Everett and Grace Rodebaugh. The Rodebaughs reintroduced native trees and meadows and constructed a series of ponds in the valley beneath the farmhouse.

In 1964, Everett Rodebaugh founded the Green Valleys Association to protect five watersheds draining 151 square miles of northern Chester County. In 1997 the Rodebaughs conveyed Welkinweir to the Green Valleys Association for use as a headquarters and educational center.

Chester County

Distance from Philadelphia
- 37 miles
Phone Number
- (610) 469-4990
Website
- www.greenvalleys.org/welk.html
Admission Fee
- Adults (17 & up) - $5.00
  Youth - $3.00
Directions
- Welkinweir is west of Phoenixville. From the intersection of Routes 23 and 100, take Route 100 south for 1.1 miles. Make a right on Prizer Road. Follow for .8 a mile to Welkinweir on the left. The Visitor Entrance is the second of three access points and is marked by a sign.

The Walks

A woodland trail loops around the 162-acre nature sanctuary, leading through wetlands, ponds, and meadows. The trail, which takes about an hour to complete, can be narrow and overgrown through the back of the property. For longer walks, the Welkinweir trail features a short connector to the *Horse-Shoe Trail*, which skirts the property on two sides.

This is hilly property, especially in the backstretch of the loop. Some of the meadow trails are shaved stalks which are rough on your pet's paws.

Trail Sense: The West Trail Entrance begins at the parking lot and the trail is blazed in white. It is not a complete loop and there is a property map available to navigate through the developed areas.

Dog Friendliness

Dogs are welcome along all the trails here.

Traffic

The small admission fee at Welkinweir helps keep crowds down.

Canine Swimming

Although the West Branch of Beaver Run is not deep enough for doggie dipping, it engorges into several ponds on the property.

Trail Time

More than an hour.

"What counts is not necessarily the size of the dog in the fight but the size of the fight in the dog."
-Dwight D. Eisenhower

34

Pennypack Park

The Park

Pennypack Park gets its name from the Lenni-Lenape Indians who hunted and fished along the creek for hundreds of years. The name means "dead deep water." Pennypack Park has often been called the Cradle of American Ornithology due to work done here by John James Audubon and Alexander Wilson. The City of Philadelphia established the park in 1905 to insure protection of 1600 acres of woodlands and wetlands.

Philadelphia County

Distance from Philadelphia
- 9 miles
Phone Number
- None
Website
- www.balford.com/fopp/
Admission Fee
- None
Directions
- Pennypack Park is in northeast Philadelphia, stretching from the eastern border of Montgomery County almost to the Delaware River. Parking is generally available near the major north-south cross roads through the park.

The Walks

Pennypack Park is the younger, rougher brother to the Wissahickon Gorge. The adventurous canine hiker can search out miles of little-used side trails, many quite narrow, off the main 18-mile multi-use trail. The land around the Pennypack Creek is modestly hilly, although you can walk for a long time without noticing it. The multi-use trail is paved. Watch for paw-slicing glass on some of the dirt trails.

Trail Sense: Pennypack Park is for the explorer; there are no maps or trail blazes or mapboards, save for the general route of the multi-use trail. Let the dog lead the way.

Dog Friendliness

Dogs are welcome in Pennypack Park.

Traffic

Pennypack is a busy city park with a few side excursions available for solitude seekers.

Canine Swimming

The fall line of the Pennypack Creek is in the park south of Frankford Avenue where the last set of rapids play out and the water drops to the level of its final destination, the Delaware River. After the fall line, the tides change the swimming pools from shallow to deep and back again in a twice-repeated daily cycle.

Trail Time

More than an hour.

35

Evansburg State Park

The Park

This land was part of William Penn's American Province purchased from the Lenni Lenape Nation in 1684. The area developed rapidly; by 1714 settlers were sending goods to Philadelphia via the Skippack (from the Lenape word for "wetland") Pike. The agrarian ways of the Mennonites in the Skippack Valley began to evaporate in the years following World War II and plans began for setting aside the land that became Evansburg State Park. The park officially opened for public use on June 28, 1974.

Montgomery County

Distance from Philadelphia
 - 30 miles
Phone Number
 - (610) 409-1150
Website
 - www.dcnr.state.pa.us/
   stateparks/evansburg.htm
Admission Fee
 - None
Directions
 - Evansburg State Park is east of Collegeville. From Route 29, pick up Germantown Pike across the Perkiomen Bridge. Make a left on Skippack Creek Road; continue straight onto May Hill Road into the Main Park Area.

The Walks

Although Evansburg comprises more than 3,000 acres, most of the property is set aside for hunting and trapping. There are 6 miles of hiking trails, primarily on the *Skippack Creek Loop Trail* which is essentially two linear trails on either side of the Skippack Creek. This is mostly easy walking with some moderate ups and downs, although the trail on the far side of the Skippack Creek can rise some 100 feet above the water. On the Main Park Area side the trail is wider and flatter, the far side is woodsier and more scenic. Another 15 miles of walking is available on equestrian trails.

Trail Sense: Trails are blazed and a map is available but the Skippack Loop never leaves the creek for more than a few yards.

Dog Friendliness

All trails are open to dogs.

Traffic

Although there are not a wide variety of trails to choose from in Evansburg State Park, the traffic load is not overbearing. You will not, however, find the solitude of other parks here.

Canine Swimming

The Skippack Creek is seldom deep enough for sustained dog-paddling and there are no ponds in the park.

Trail Time

More than an hour.

"Money will buy a pretty good dog but it won't buy the wag of his tail."

-Josh Billings

36

Bellevue State Park

The Park

Bellevue is the former estate of William duPont, Jr., where he hosted America's greatest tennis players and stabled his Foxcatcher Farms horses. Five Kentucky Derby horses worked on the track used now by cyclists, joggers and dog walkers.

The Walks

The main attraction at Bellevue State Park is the 9-furlong (1 1/8 miles) training track. It is wide, flat and exceedingly pleasant to walk with your dog. You can also cobble together a canine hike around the perimeter of the park by following bike and horse trails. These lead you to community gardens, a small nature preserve, the paddocks and several estate buildings.

Trail Sense: A ranger has never needed to come to the rescue of a lost dog walker in Bellevue State Park. An excellent map is available just the same.

New Castle County

Distance from Philadelphia
- 22 miles
Phone Number
- (302) 577-3390
Website
- www.destateparks.com/bvsp/bvsp.htm
Admission Fee
- Fee charge daily from Memorial Day-Labor Day and weekends in May, September and October
Directions
- The main entrance is just north of the Marsh Road exit of I-95 on Carr Road, between Marsh Road and Silverside Road.

Dog Friendliness

Dogs are welcome at the Bellevue State Park.

Traffic

The training track is popular with joggers, cyclists and baby strollers.

Canine Swimming

There is a small pond in the center of the training track but it is more for those feeding the geese and dropping a fishing line than doggie aquatics.

Trail Time

Less than an hour.

37

Indian Orchard / Linvill Trails

The Park

In 1986, Middletown Township began preserving significant portions of open space in Middletown in recognition of the Township's Tricentennial. These trails were carved from 157 acres of property acquired from the Linvill family.

The Walks

The *Indian Orchard Trail*, blazed in yellow, rolls through a woodland of mature hardwoods and conifers, crossing five bridges along its one-mile length. The *Linvill Trail* covers 3 1/2 miles over two sections; one, a long perimeter loop around the pasturelands and orchards, the other a fish-hook trail behind Linvilla Orchard.

Delaware County

Distance from Philadelphia
 - 21 miles
Phone Number
 - None
Website
 - None
Admission Fee
 - None
Directions
 - The trails are south of Lima, just off Route 352 (Middletown Road). The parking lot for the Indian Orchard Trail is at the end of Copes Lane on the western side of Route 352. To reach the Linville Trail from Route 1, make a right on West Knowlton Road and take your first right on Linville Road to the parking lot.

A short spur connects the two trails. These trails are easy hiking, with the Linvill Trail the flatter of the two. Indian Orchard features some sporty ups and downs. Take caution on the *Farm Fields Trail* which is sometimes cut from the crop stalks, leaving tiny spears that can injure a pet's paws.

Trail Sense: The trails are marked but are not always distinct when the blazes are on young trees in regenerating woods. The best trail map in Delaware County is available from the township office but not at the trailhead.

Dog Friendliness

Dogs are welcome along all the trails here.

Traffic

There is little competition for space on these trails.

Canine Swimming

Crum Run intercepts the Indian Orchard Trail several times although it is not deep enough for a full swim. The most water you'll encounter on the Linville Trail is at the Hidden Hollow Swim Club, which doesn't welcome dogs in its pools.

Trail Time

More than an hour.

38

Riverbend Education Center

The Park

The Riverbend story begins 300,000,000 years ago when a crack in the rock known as the Rosemont Fault turned what would become known as the Schuylkill River a full 90 degrees. The first settlers came to the area in the 1500s when the Lenni-Lenape Indians began planting vegetables in an area known as "Indian Fields." In 1904, Howard Wood, brother of steel magnate Alan Wood, created a 52-acre farm inside the river's elbow. Three generations later, in 1974, his descendents deeded half of the farm to serve as a wildlife refuge known as Riverbend Environmental Education Center.

Montgomery County

Distance from Philadelphia
- 12 miles
Phone Number
- (610) 527-5234
Website
- www.gladwyne.com/riverbend/
Admission Fee
- None
Directions
- Riverbend is in Gladwyne. From the Blue Route (I-476) North, take Exit 6A for Conshohocken, Route 23 East. Make a left on Spring Mill Road, continue past the Philadelphia Country Club and bear left at the end of the road to the Education Center parking lot.

The Walks

The feature trail at Riverbend, amidst two miles of hiking, is the *Aloha Trail* that circles the perimeter of the property. Unfortunately the walk is marred by the relentless pounding of traffic on the Schuylkill Expressway below. Look for *Fiveleaf Akebia,* an invasive plant that covers everything on the hillside above the roadway. The other trails are short connecting spurs of only several minutes duration. Avoid the *Jack-in-the-Pulpit* and *Poplar* trails- they can be overgrown. Another hike here is *Sid Thayer's Trail,* a linear trail on private property also plagued by traffic noise. Riverbend is situated on the knob of a hill and there is little flat walking to be had here.

Trail Sense: There is a hand-painted mapboard at the parking lot for orientation. On the trails there are signposts at junctions. The Aloha Trail is blazed in red and marked by trail signs which are handy through the tricky residential passage.

Dog Friendliness

Dogs are welcome along all the trails here.

Traffic

Aside from school groups during the week there is little competition on the trails at Riverbend.

Canine Swimming

Riverbend sports the smallest pond in the tri-state area, alongside the *Bluebird Trail*. Although scarcely ten feet across, smaller dogs can motor around and larger ones can drop in to cool off.

Trail Time

Less than an hour.

39

Silver Lake Park

The Park

The centerpiece of Silver Lake Park is the Silver Lake Nature Center, opened by the Bucks County Department of Parks and Recreation in 1960. Within its 235 protected acres are two rare habitats, a coastal plain forest (Delhaas Woods) and an unglaciated bog, as well as two animals and 11 plants on the Pennsylvania species of special concern list. The Nature Center is flanked by two small lakes, the secluded Magnolia Lake and the landscaped Silver Lake.

Bucks County

Distance from Philadelphia
- 22 miles
Phone Number
- (215) 785-1177
Website
- www.bucksnet.com/ silverlake/
Admission Fee
- None
Directions
- Silver Lake Park is on Bath Road off of Route 13 in Bristol.

The Walks

Ducking onto the quiet, scented trails of the Silver Lake Nature Center provides a complete escape from the hustle and bustle of surrounding Lower Bucks County. The well-groomed paths give way to boardwalks over marshy ground and small streams as they lead into the high swamp grass. A paved bicycle trail leads most of the way around Silver Lake.

Across Bath Road is a small opening in the trees that leads to several miles of dirt trails in the 181 acres of wooded wetlands in Delhaas Woods. All the walking at Silver Lake is across level terrain.

Trail Sense: There is a map that identifies the major regions of the park but no trail map. The trails in Delhaas Woods are unmapped and unmarked.

Dog Friendliness

Dogs are permitted on trails in the park and nature center.

Traffic

Silver Lake is a popular destination for strollers and wildlife observers. There is less competition for the trails in Delhaas Woods.

Canine Swimming

There is access to Silver Lake for a doggie dip.

Trail Time

Less than an hour.

*"He is very imprudent, a dog is. He never makes it
his business to inquire whether you are in the right
or in the wrong, never bothers as to whether you are
going up or down upon life's ladder, never asks
whether you are rich or poor, silly or wise,
sinner or saint.""*

-Jerome K. Jerome

40

Crow's Woods

Park History

The area was first settled in 1682 but things didn't really get going until 21-year old Elizabeth Haddon arrived in 1701 to establish her father's claims here. It wasn't until 1875 that Haddonfield Borough was officially established and the natural area south of town has been known as Crow's Woods for nearly as long. For years part of the area was used as a landfill which was converted into playing fields following the 1967 construction of the PATCO Hi-Speed Line which abuts the park. Today, the grounds at Crow's Woods encompass more than 65 acres.

The Walks

Crow's Woods packs plenty of topographical diversity into its short, intermingling trails. In fact, so many dog walkers have come from outside Haddonfield to enjoy the park's ravines and hills that borough commissioners have considered imposing a "use tag" system similar to New Jersey beaches for non-residents.

The wide, soft dirt paths wind through dense woodlands of scrub oak, pitch pine and mountain laurel. An asphalt jogging track around the perimeter of the sports fields is also available.

Trail Sense: Three trails are blazed in blue, yellow and white but any route can be improvised in the compact Crow's Woods without fear of becoming lost.

Dog Friendliness

Dogs are permitted off leash in the woods but must be restrained near the playing fields.

Traffic

In addition to dog walkers, Crow's Woods is popular with mountain bikers.

Canine Swimming

There are small swimming holes in the woods that are more suited for a refreshing splash than sustained dog paddling.

Trail Time

Less than an hour.

41

Lorimer
Nature Preserve

Park History

The nature preserve, managed by the Open Land Conservancy, is named for George Horimer Lorimer, longtime editor of the *Saturday Evening Post*. Lorimer, a resident of Wyncote, was a passionate conservationist during his lifetime.

The Walks

The Lorimer Preserve is an ideal spot for a walk of less than an hour. The short, interconnecting maze of trails offer a pleasing mix of fields and woods. The walking is easy throughout with many flat streches, especially in the fields. The paths are almost all paw-pleasing grass.

Trail Sense: There are no maps and no blazed trails so your route is left to your imagination. You can criss-cross the property and still find your way back to the parking lot without calling for a St. Bernard-led rescue party.

Dog Friendliness

It sometimes seems as if this park was designed for dog walkers.

Chester County

Distance from Philadelphia
- 26 miles
Phone Number
- None
Website
- None
Admission Fee
- None
Directions
- Lorimer Nature Preserve is in Tredyffrin Township. The main entrance is on North Valley Road, north of Swedesford Road. Turn right into the small parking lot up the hill from the bridge across Valley Creek.

Traffic

There are no bikes and no horses at Lorimer.

Canine Swimming

In addition to the Bonus pond (above) there is a larger pond on the property as well which is also excellent for dog swimming when there is adequate rainfall.

Trail Time

Less than an hour.

42

Ashland Nature Center

The Park

A mill operated here as early as 1715. Since 1964, when the Delaware Nature Society was founded, 200 acres at Ashland Nature Center have been preserved for the conservation and study of natural resources.

The Walks

There are four self-guiding nature trails here, each a loop between .8 and 1.3 miles. *Sugarbush* and *Treetop* trails explore the wooded hillside beyond the Ashland Covered Bridge, built in the days before the Civil War; the adjoining *Succession* and *Flood Plain* trails visit meadow, marsh, pond and forest. There is a good deal of hillwalking at Ashland, save for the benign Flood Plain Trail. The trails are natural - dirt covered in the woods; grass in the meadows.

Trail Sense: The trails and interpretive stops, over 30 on some trails, are well-marked.

Dog Friendliness

Dogs are welcome at the Ashland Nature Center.

Traffic

No bikes or horses compete on the trails at Ashland Nature Center.

New Castle County

Distance from Philadelphia
- 37 miles
Phone Number
- (302) 239-2334
Website
- delawarenaturesociety.org/ashland.htm
Admission Fee
- Yes, to use the trails
Directions
- Ashland Nature Center is in Hockessin, on Barley Mill Road, between Creek Road (Route 82) and Brackenville Road.

Canine Swimming

Birch Run and the Red Clay Creek flow through the property. Neither is deep enough to dog paddle in.

Trail Time

More than an hour.

Answers to boxed questions:

1. *Glacial runoff carved Delaware's valleys from a high plateau.*
2. *Oak and beech.*
3. *Eroded soil carried downstream from far-off mountains.*
4. *Schists of rock were folded in by intense pressure deep in the earth.*
5. *The trees, usually tulip poplars that compete with sycamores as the burliest in Eastern forests, are shade intolerant and are constantly striving for the sun.*

43

Tamanend
Community Park

The Park

In an elaborate treaty ceremony in his Philadelphia house in 1683, William Penn purchased all the land between Pennypack and Neshaminy Creeks. In turning over the lands, Chief Tamanend, a Lenape Sachem, declared the treaty of friendship would endure "as long as the grass is green and the rivers flow." Scarcely a half century later Penn's descendents had broken the treaty and driven the Lenape nation from Pennsylvania. A wooden figurehead likeness of Chief Tamanend graced the *USS Delaware* and eventually wound up on the grounds of the United States Naval Academy.

Bucks County

Distance from Philadelphia
- 25 miles
Phone Number
- None
Website
- None
Admission Fee
- None
Directions
- Tamanend Community Park is located in Southampton. The entrance is on Second Street Pike (Route 232) between Bristol Road and Street Road (Route 132).

This land was farmed for more than two centuries until the 1940s when William Long established Southampton Nurseries. In addition to the commercial stock, Long introduced exotic species of trees and shrubs as well. In 1975 Upper Southampton Township and the Centennial School District jointly purchased the 109-acre Tamanend Park for nearly one million dollars.

The Walks

For a small township park wedged between a rail line and a busy roadway, Tamanend sports a surprising variety of canine hikes. The *Red Arrowhead Trail* skirts the perimeter of the property for 2.3 miles and the *Blue Arrowhead* and *Yellow*

Arrowhead trails are interior loops of about one mile in length. The dirt trails are generally wide and easy to negotiate.

Two short, special trails are the stars at Tamanend, however. The *History Trail* interprets the heritage of the property and structures remaining from by-gone days. Highlights include the William Penn Treaty Elm, a fifth generation offspring of the great elm tree under which Penn negotiated with the Lenni Lenape, and a Sequoia *Giganteum*, a species of mountain redwood originally found only in China and California. The *Glenn Sokol Trail* is a quiet nature trail created in honor of a local naturalist.

Trail Sense: Tamanend is not for the directionally-challenged. Although there are rudimentary maps and trails are blazed, the primary tool for getting around Tamanend is printed turn-by-turn directions in the trail brochures.

Dog Friendliness

All trails are open to dogs.

Traffic

This is a compact, busy park and the trails touch on many of the recreation areas in the park.

Canine Swimming

There is some dog paddling to be had in the small Klinger Pond but this is not a canine swimmer's paradise.

Trail Time

More than an hour.

44

Springfield Trail

The Park

The creation of trails in most parks seems fairly obvious - use established animal paths or fire roads. But the Springfield Trail, linking four parks in a 5-mile loop roughly corralled by Woodland Avenue, the Blue Route and the SEPTA Trolley line, required vision and imagination of Springfield Township and private property owners in 1969 to bring into existence.

The Walks

There are no shortcuts on the *Springfield Trail*; once you set off you sign on for the whole five miles. The strongest segment is from Jane Lownes Park to Smedley Park as the trail hugs the Crum Creek, often from a scenic ridge 100 feet above the water. Although it's noisy due to the adjacent Blue Route (the trail twice brings you directly beneath the superstructure) this is the walk to take if you decide to do an out-and-back. The hike along the trolley line from Smedley to Thompson Park is a wild and wooly excursion that brings you across train tracks, through dry creek beds, past ferns and wild roses and more. The quietest stretch on the Springfield Trail is the narrow trail along Whiskey Run. There is also sidewalking along Woodland Road to complete the loop. This is a healthy workout; none of the climbs will bring you to your knees but they keep coming with dogged regularity.

Delaware County

Distance from Philadelphia
- 10 miles
Phone Number
- None
Website
- None
Admission Fee
- None
Directions
- The easiest access is at Lownes Park and Smedley Park. The entrance for Smedley Park is on Baltimore Pike, just east of Exit 2 of the Blue Route. Park in the Paper Mill Road lot across the trolley tracks and pick up the Trail at the Comfort Station. Lownes Park is off Route 320 with street parking along Kennerly Road.

Trail Sense: The yellow-blazed trail is well-marked through the woods but can use some touching up in the civilized areas around the trolley tracks and the roads. There is no map so you are dependent on these painted rectangles. The Springfield Trail is plagued by trail-obliterating fallen trees; even some of the blazed trees have collapsed into the creek.

Dog Friendliness

Dogs are welcome all along the Springfield Trail but there is automobile traffic in places.

Traffic

Although there are many access points to the Springfield trail loop it is possible to achieve a sense of isolation.

Canine Swimming

There are streams everywhere along the Springfield Trail but seldom is the water even a foot deep.

Trail Time

More than an hour.

113

45

State Game Lands #43

The Park

Three segments of these public lands, totalling 2,150 acres, lie in northwest Chester County. The most accessible - and scenic - of the three is at Saint Peters. Once known as the Falls of French Creek and a famous local tourist destination, Saint Peters was named for the town church when the post office moved away.

The Walks

The *Horse-Shoe Trail* cuts through the Saint Peters and Pine Swamp Tracts. The Saint Peters walk is heavily wooded; the Pine Swamp walk leads through a scruffy meadow on old access roads through light woods at the edge of fields. There are many other short interconnecting trails at Saint Peters, crossing over small streams and an abandoned rail line. The rolling terrain never gets oppressive and the walking is easy throughout.

Trail Sense: The Horse-Shoe Trail is blazed but there is no trail map to untwine the maze of trails under the trees at Saint Peters. The Horse-Shoe Trail has no branches as it slices through the Pine Swamp tract.

Chester County

Distance from Philadelphia
- 44 miles
Phone Number
- None
Website
- None
Admission Fee
- None
Directions
- The parking lot at Saint Peters is on Saint Peters Road, north of Route 23 (Ridge Road). It is behind the buildings on the left, at the northern edge of town. In Pine Swamp there is a small, unmarked parking lot on Harmonyville Road, east of Route 345 (Pine Swamp Road).

Dog Friendliness

Dogs are welcome along all the trails here.

Traffic

Save for maps, there is nothing to lead visitors to this parcel of Pennsylvania state game lands. No signs, no mapboards. You should have these woods to yourself.

Canine Swimming

French Creek rushes downhill through the property, pooling into an ideal swimming pond just south of the parking lot. Pine Creek can be accessed at Pine Swamp from the bridge near the parking lot.

Trail Time

More than an hour.

"Children are for people who
can't have dogs."
-Anonymous

46

Nockamixon State Park

The Park

Once a prominent settlement for the Lenni Lenape Indians, Nockamixon State Park was planned and developed by the U.S. Army Corps of Engineers with the damming of the Tohickon Creek. The park officially opened in 1973 and the resulting Lake Nockamixon has become the premier destination for boating in southeast Pennsylvania. Combined with the adjacent State Game Land #157, more than 7,000 acres - the largest open space in Bucks County - is available for public recreation.

The Walks

The Indians called the land "nocha-miska-ing" - "at the place of soft soil." Little

Bucks County

Distance from Philadelphia
  - 47 miles
Phone Number
  - (215) 529-7300
Website
  - www.dcnr.state.pa.us/
    stateparks/nock.htm
Admission Fee
  - None
Directions
  - Lake Nockamixon is in northcentral Bucks County. The main entrance to the park is located on Route 563 and is reached from the south on Route 413/412. To reach Haycock Mountain in State Game Lands #157 go west 1.1 miles on Route 563 from the junction with Route 412. Turn onto Top Rock Road and go .6 miles to the parking lot on the left.

has changed in the 400 years since. These low, often water-level trails are indeed soft and, many times, downright squishy. There are more than 20 miles of the soft equestrian trails and a paved 2.8-mile bicycle trail skirts the shoreline as well. A 21-mile circumnavigation of Lake Nockamixon can be parsed together with bridle paths, trails and back roads.

A unique experience awaits the athletic dog at Haycock Mountain in State Game Land #157. The mountain is essentially a ridge of diabase boulders and the trail to the top calls for almost continuous rock-hopping, a technique called bouldering. The basaltic rock provides incredible traction for boot and paw. A narrow, red-blazed and stone-strewn trail leads uphill from the parking lot to the boulder field. After that the trails are marked by white and blue blazes but the way to the top is frequently obfuscated by scores of fallen trees. This bouldering is a walk unlike any other in the region.

Trail Sense: A park map is available to provide a sketchy view of where you are rather than detailed routes.

Dog Friendliness

Dogs are welcome in the park; approximately 3,000 acres are open to dog training from Labor Day to March 31.

Traffic

Off-road biking is not permitted. Outside the recreational area, there is little trail competition at Nockamixon.

Canine Swimming

The trails seldom touch the densely wooded shores of Lake Nockamixon but there is good swimming when the chance comes.

Trail Time

More than an hour.

"Properly trained, a man can be dog's best friend."
-Corey Ford

47

Main Line Colleges

The Park

Several private colleges along the Main Line welcome responsible dog owners to visit campus.

The Walks

Bryn Mawr College Arboretum. This English-landscape style campus mixes massive trees with its gothic buildings. The campus grounds were designed by the firm of Frederick Law Olmsted, architects of many of America's greatest parks.

Haverford College Arboretum. The college dates to 1833, making it the oldest institution of higher learning with Quaker roots in the country. There are two walking choices here: a nearly three-mile loop around the perimeter of the campus (you'll barely see any school buildings) or an Arboretum tour highlighting 33 special trees.

Rosemont College. At 56 acres, the smallest of the Main Line grounds, Rosemont offers a quiet walk around the knob of a hill. At the center of campus is *Rathalla*, resplendent with its French Renaissance turrets. The original house on the Sinnott Estate, it once contained all college activities.

Delaware County

Distance from Philadelphia
- 13 miles
Phone Number
- None
Website
- None
Admission Fee
- None
Directions
- From east to west: Haverford is on Route 30. Follow the signs to the Visitor Parking Lot where you can pick up a campus map and the trailhead. Bryn Mawr is three blocks north of Route 30 via Roberts Road. Parking is on the street. Rosemont College is on Montgmery Avenue; visitor parking is left of the entrance. Villanova is spread across Routes 30 and 321. The main parking is opposite the campus on Route 30.

Villanova Arboretum. The oldest and largest Catholic university in Pennsylvania formally dedicated its arboretum in 1993 - more than 100 years after many of the school's 1,500 trees were well-established. The trees are easily identified from the paths.

Trail Sense: Bryn Mawr, Haverford and Villanova have numerous map boards. The only formal trail is at Haverford and is actually 3/4 of a loop that must be completed by ducking through some back parking lots; a campus map is available.

Dog Friendliness

Dogs and college go together like football and falling leaves.

Traffic

Most of the campus walking can be accomplished with a minimum of street crossing.

Canine Swimming

There are small streams at Haverford and Rosemont but no canine swimming.

Trail Time

Generally less than an hour; although you can spend more than an hour at Haverford on the *Nature Trail*.

*"Dog. A kind of additional or subsidiary Deity
designed to catch the overflow and surplus
of the world's worship."*
                                        -Ambrose Bierce

48

Marsh Creek State Park

The Park

To counter frequent flooding in the Brandywine Creek watershed, plans for Marsh Creek Dam began in 1955. Work on the 89-foot earthen dam began in 1970. In 1974 the lake began to fill and six months later 535 acres of what used to be Milford Mills were under up to 73 feet of water. Gone were 42 residences and more than 70 old barns and other structures.

The Walks

Marsh Creek Lake dominates the 1,705 acres of the park. There is no hiking at the main entrance on the east side of the lake. All the hiking - six miles worth - lies on the western shores. The main loop (*Bridle Trail*) is

Chester County

Distance from Philadelphia
- 37 miles
Phone Number
- (610) 458-5119
Website
- www.dcnr.state.pa.us/ stateparks/m-crek.htm
Admission Fee
- None
Directions
- The hiking trails at Marsh Creek are reached from Route 282 (Creek Road). From the south, make a right on Reeds Road North. From the north, make a left on Lyndell Road. Both feed into Marsh Creek Road and the parking lot.

interjected with three inner loops. The trail is on a hill overlooking the lake but water views are few. The trails are heavily wooded.

The terrain is hilly leading from the trailhead but easy walking once the high hill is scaled; down the opposite side of the hill the trail hooks into an old railbed along the East Branch of the Brandywine Creek. This stretch of trail, the prettiest in the park, is flat. The trails are mostly dirt although there are long patches of rocky ground on the slopes that are tough on foot and paw.

Trail Sense: There are many more trails at Marsh Creek State Park than are indicated on the trail map. An occasional sign pops up to inspire confidence and some blazes but mostly you and the dog are on your own.

Dog Friendliness

Dogs are welcome along the hiking trails here.

Traffic

Marsh Creek is a heavily used park for all manner of recreation. Don't expect to have these trails to yourself.

Canine Swimming

Accessed from the parking lot, Marsh Creek Lake offers the best lake swimming in Chester County; the Brandywine Creek here is usually too shallow for anything more than splashing.

Trail Time

More than an hour.

49

Lums Pond State Park

The Park

In the early 1800s the Army Corps of Engineers dammed the St. Georges Creek to hold water for the locks of the original Chesapeake and Delaware Canal. The result is Delaware's largest freshwater pond, a 200-acre water playground for boaters, fishermen, swimmers - and dogs.

The Walks

The *Swamp Forest Trail* at Lums Pond circumnavigates the water and covers over seven miles. Along the way you will hike through woods and fields and cross 26 bridges. Look for the tooth-work of the active colony of beavers at Lums Pond. There are some short climbs, especially on the eastern shore, but this is essentially a flat romp around the lake. If three hours of steady trekking with your dog isn't your hiking menu, however, don't attempt this trip. Lums Pond also features over 10 miles of dirt and grass multi-purpose trails for horse, bikes and dog walkers and a unique .1-mile "sensory trail."

Trail Sense: The trail is not always marked and can get confusing through recreational areas and the disk golf course.

New Castle County

Distance from Philadelphia
  - 43 miles
Phone Number
  - (302) 368-6989
Website
  - www.destateparks.com/ lpsp/lpsp.htm
Admission Fee
  - Fee charge daily from Memorial Day-Labor Day and weekends in May, September and October
Directions
  - The way in to Lums Pond is on Howell School Road between Red Lion Road (Route 71) and Route 896. The entrance to the Dog Training Area is east of the Main Entrance on Buck Jersey Road.

Dog Friendliness

Dogs are allowed on the Lums Pond Trail but not on the swimming beach. There is an off-leash Dog Training Area in the northeast finger of the lake.

Traffic

There will be more traffic out on the water than on most places along this trail. There is trail-sharing with horses on only a few short segments of the Swamp Forest Trail.

Canine Swimming

All the time along the trail.

Trail Time

More than an hour.

50

Taylor Wildlife Preserve

The Park

In 1720 Joshua Wright purchased land along the Delaware River known to the local Indians as "the island" since it often remained dry during the periodic flooding of the river, which rises and falls as much as five feet between high and low tides. The land has remained in his family ever since. In 1975 Sylvia and Joshua Taylor donated 89 acres of their 130-acre property to the New Jersey National Lands Trust and opened the Taylor Wildlife Preserve to the public.

Burlington County

Distance from Philadelphia
- 12 miles
Phone Number
- None
Website
- None
Admission Fee
- None
Directions
- Taylor Wildlife Preserve is east of Riverton, off River Road (Route 543). The main entrance is on Taylors Lane and the trails can also be accessed from Inman Street.

The Walks

One of the few remaining accessible open spaces remaining along the heavily industrialized Delaware River is at Taylor Wildlife Preserve. As it is, the preserve is squeezed against the water by four neighboring industrial parks. A 12-step interpretive trail has been carved around a vibrant freshwater marsh. For the most part the trails are dirt and stony. Several benches have been provided overlooking the marsh and the Delaware River. The walk along the river is one of the longest in the area and dogs can easily reach the water for a swim.

Trail Sense: Grassy areas can become overgrown and yellow-backed directional markers have been strategically placed.

Dog Friendliness

Dogs are welcome in the wildlife preserve.

Traffic

There are no horses or bikes to dodge here.

Canine Swimming

There is easy access to the Delaware River for good dog paddling.

Trail Time

Less than an hour.

51

Warwick County Park

The Park

The woodlands in Warwick County Park's 455 acres provided much of the timber for charcoal used in the American iron industry. The land was an original grant to Samuel Nutt in 1718, who took to mining the property. By 1738 the Warwick Furnace was established and it was to be one of the most substantial in the American colonies. The first Franklin Stove was cast here and the Warwick Cannon helped win the Revolution. Charcoal hearths chiseled into the steep slopes can still be seen flanking some trails. The park was dedicated in 1973.

Chester County

Distance from Philadelphia
- 47 miles
Phone Number
- (610) 469-1916
Website
- None
Admission Fee
- None
Directions
- Warwick County Park is in Knauertown, on Route 23, four miles west of Route 100. The main park entrance is located on County Park Road and parking for the North Loop Trail is on Mt. Pleasant Road, east of the main entrance.

The Walks

The premier walk in Warwick is the *Charcoal Trail Loop*, a narrow, rocky, mile-long loop up and down the slopes of the French Creek Valley. The *North Loop Trail*, designed like a long lasso, is a pleasant woods-and-field walk, much of it on the old bed of the Sowbelly Railroad. Two of the *Horse-Shoe Trail's* 133 miles bisect the park and there is a 1/2-mile *Adirondack Trail* where you can test your ability to identify the trees and shrubs commonly found in an Eastern hardwood forest. The trail access from the Coventry Road parking lot is overgrown and provides access only to the French Creek South Branch, but not the rest of the park. There are many long stretches of flat terrain and easy walking but the Charcoal Trail will give your dog a cardiac workout.

Trail Sense: The trails are blazed, save for the North Loop, and a trail map is available.

Dog Friendliness

Dogs are welcome along all the trails here.

Traffic

The trails won't be clogged in this park in rural Chester County.

Canine Swimming

There is very little water at Warwick; none at all along the Charcoal Trail and minimal access to the French Creek elsewhere. There is, however, a pretty, fleeting encounter with the creek on the North Loop, west of the Conifer Field.

Trail Time

More than an hour.

"Happiness is dog-shaped."
-Chapman Pincher

52

Cooper River Park

The Park

People began settling along the Cooper and Newton creeks in the 1690s as the waterways became busy conduits for goods to and from a young Philadelphia. Through the decades the free flow of water became strangled by all manner of debris and waste tumbling from the industrializing banks. In 1936 workers from the Works Project Administration waded into the putrid Cooper River swamp to build a dam, shove around mountains of dirt and shaped the creek into the slender lake that is the centerpiece of Cooper River Park.

Camden County

Distance from Philadelphia
- 7 miles
Phone Number
- None
Website
- None
Admission Fee
- None
Directions
- Cooper River Park is in Pennsauken, traversed by Park Drive North and Park Drive South. Access is from Cuthbert Boulevard to the east and Crescent Boulevard (Route 130) to the west.

The Walks

A 3.8-mile paved pathway loops around the active lake. The serpentine route features almost continually unobstructed views of the water, which on most days will be sprinkled with sailors from the Cooper River Yacht Club on the south shore. Long stretches of the walk, especially in the eastern end of the park, are bereft of recreational activity, leaving you alone with other dog walkers and joggers. A number of war memorial monuments and statues grace the route.

Trail Sense: There is no map available but the park boundaries are only several yards from the lake on both sides.

Dog Friendliness

At the far eastern shore of the lake, at the terminus of N. Shore Drive is a designated Pooch Park with two small enclosed dog runs, one for dogs over 30 pounds and another for smaller dogs. The lighted facility is open daily from 6 a.m. to 10 p.m., although the lights are more ornamental than functional.

Traffic

Cooper River is a busy urban park.

Canine Swimming

There is access to the water at many points along the paved trail.

Trail Time

Less than an hour.

"My dog is worried about the economy because Alpo is up to 99 cants a can. That's almost $7.00 in dog money."

-Joe Weinstein

53

Springton Manor Park

The Park

Springton Manor was originally an 8,313-acre parcel set aside by William Penn in 1701. The land has been farmed for almost three centuries and lives today as a demonstration farm. A small forge also operated here for much of the 18th century. Abraham McIlvaine built the main house in 1833. Springton Manor Farm is listed on the National Register of Historic Places for its importance in architecture, agriculture and conservation.

Chester County

Distance from Philadelphia
- 40 miles
Phone Number
- (610) 942-2450
Website
- None
Admission Fee
- None
Directions
- Springton Manor is northwest of Downingtown. Take Route 282, Creek Road, out of Downingtown for five miles and make a left on Springton Road. The entrance to the park is up the hill on the left.

The Walks

The *Indian Run Trail* loops around the entire property - evenly divided between field and woods hiking. In July the southwestern edge of the field is bursting with the most accessible red raspberries in Chester County. There is also available a winding 1/3-mile *Penn Oak Interpretive Nature Trail*. The farmland sweeps down a long hillside providing gentle climbs and sparkling views; the lowlands surrounding Indian Run are flat. The Indian Run loop is dirt and grass with some wood chips under foot; the Nature Trail is paved with macadam.

Trail Sense. The loop is the only trail on the property. Although it is not marked, it is easy to follow. There is a map available.

Dog Friendliness

Dogs are welcome along all the trails here.

Traffic

Most likely you will be enjoying the sweeping panoramic views of the countryside by yourself.

Canine Swimming

The Farmer's Pond, at the edge of the Nature Trail, was built in 1896 as an additional water source for crops and live-stock. The shallow-running Indian Run is good for splashing.

Trail Time

More than an hour.

54
Peace Valley Park

The Park

Ancient earthquakes once rumbled along a fault line under the north branch of the Neshaminy Creek creating mineral veins of zinc, gold, copper, silver and uranium. But mostly lead. The rich veins of lead ore - some 90% pure - were as close as five feet from the surface. Beginning in the 1860s the first of 26 mine shafts were sunk and over the next 70 years 2600 tons of ore were hauled from the innards of the earth before the high cost of pumping out water closed the mines forever. In the 1970s the Neshaminy Creek was dammed and the main pit flooded. The resulting 356-acre lake was named *Galena*, Latin for "lead ore." Today, Peace Valley Park surrounding Lake Galena includes over 1500 acres, making it one of the largest parks in southeastern Pennsylvania.

Bucks County

Distance from Philadelphia
 - 39 miles
Phone Number
 - (215) 348-6114
Website
 - www.cronancomputer.com/bcparks/pvpark/
Admission Fee
 - None
Directions
 - Peace Valley Park is 3 miles north of Doylestown off Route 313, between Ferry Road and New Galena Road.

The Walks

The main hike at Peace Valley is a paved *Hike & Bike Trail* that goes almost two-thirds of the way around Lake Galena at the western end. Dogs are not allowed on the Nature Center trails so to complete a lake circle requires a walk of more than a mile along the narrow two-lane, shoulderless New Galena Road. It is not recommended. Short, wooded bridle trails offer hiking on the south shore. There are no hills at Peace Valley.

Trail Sense: A park map is available but isn't needed for hiking around the lake.

Dog Friendliness

The prohibition of dogs in the Peace Valley Nature Center severely limits the dog-walking experience at Peace Valley.

Traffic

Peace Valley is a popular multi-use area with dogs restricted to the busiest sections of the park.

Canine Swimming

The grassy, landscaped banks of Lake Galena provide an especially inviting entry to a doggie dip, even for dogs that routinely shy away from the water.

Trail Time

More than an hour.

55

Anson B. Nixon Park

The Park

The land here, featuring a 22-foot drop in the East Branch of the Red Clay Creek, was bought in 1795 by William Chambers to build a mill. He was looking to clean wool. Chambers named his property and fine mansion "Bloomfield," in honor of Brigadier General Bloomfield who drilled 3000 troops on his brother's adjoining property in preparation for the War of 1812. The first organized school in the borough was conducted in a grove of trees here in 1830, a quarter-century before Kennett Square was incorporated. The property remained in the Chambers family for more than a century. The mansion burned and the 82-acre park was established in 1982.

Chester County

Distance from Philadelphia
 - 42 miles
Phone Number
 - (610) 388-1303
Website
 - www.ken-net.com/kennpark
Admission Fee
 - None
Directions
 - The park is located in the northeast corner of Kennett Square. From Route 1, exit onto State Street and make a right at the bottom of Miller's Hill (the first one heading into town) onto N. Walnut Street. Make a left into the park at the fork 1/4 mile ahead. You can also access the park by taking Route 82 South from Route 1 and make your first left onto Leslie Road, past the Saint Patrick Cemetery. A small parking lot is by the ballfield at the end of the lane.

The Walks

The park is essentially carved into three main segments, each featuring a walking loop. The *Beechwood Trail* in the Beech Woods slips between rare umbrella magnolias and tupelos dressed in gnarly trunks deformed from a bacterial infection. Also here is the signature Kennett Beech which stood when William Penn came from England to claim his land grant more than 300 years ago. The Bloomfield Trail circles two small ponds at the center of the property. The *Otherplace Trail,* named for the home of Cyrus Chambers, penetrates the Pine Woods on the eastern side of the park. Informal spur trails also run through Nixon Park. This is easy walking with only minor dips and rolls along the way on crushed gravel and packed dirt trails.

Trail Sense: The trails are unmarked but the many segments are short and any misdirection will not leave you lost for long. A painted map board is available in a kiosk in the parking lot.

Dog Friendliness

Dogs are welcome along all the trails here.

Traffic

Anson Nixon is a bustling town park with an active recreation area.

Canine Swimming

The Red Clay Creek is not deep enough for anything beyond splashing. The ponds are set below the level of the trails, providing tricky access at times.

Trail Time

Less than an hour.

Before I continue on and describe 63 more places to hike with your dog, let's take a minute to list some of the parks that don't allow dogs...

No Dogs!

NEW JERSEY

Burlington County

Rancocas Nature Center

Camden County

Palmyra Cove Nature Park

Gloucester County

Ceres Park
Greenwich Lake Park
Red Bank Battlefield Park
Scotland Run Park
Washington Lake Park

PENNSYLVANIA

Bucks County

Bowman's Hill Wildflower Preserve
Churchville Nature Center
Five Mile Woods Forest Preserve
Honey Hollow Environmental Education Center
Peace Valley Nature Center

Chester County

Battle of the Clouds Park
Binky Lee Preserve*
Crow's Nest Preserve*
East Whiteland Township Preserve
Great Valley Nature Center
Jenkins Arboretum
Kardon Park
Kerr Park
Sharp's/Canterbury Woods*
Stroud Preserve*
Valley Creek Park

Delaware County

Hildacy Farm*
Saw Mill Park
The Willows Park
Tyler Arboretum
Wawa Preserve*

Montgomery County

Alverthorpe Park
Briar Bush Nature Center
Gwynned Wildlife Preserve*
Lorimer County Park
Mill Grove/Audubon Wildlife Sanctuary
Morris Arboretum
Saunders Woods*
Stone Hills Wildlife Preserve
Upper Schuylkill Valley Park

indicates a park where dogs are allowed but not encouraged to visit

63 More Places To Hike With Your Dog In The Philadelphia Region

Airdrie Forest Preserve

Paoli
Chester County
corner of North Valley Road and Central Avenue off Route 30

The original Airdrie Forest is in central Scotland, where legend has it witches and warlocks once roamed. These woodlands, managed by the Open Land Conservancy, magically make the bustle of the nearby Paoli commercial district disappear. The sloping dirt trails follow hillsides overlooking a glen cut by a tributary of the Little Valley Creek. The wooded trails are well-defined but all dead-end against the preserve boundaries and the walks are short.

Alapocas Woods Park

Wilmington
New Castle County
behind the DuPont Experimental Station, off Route 141 on Alapocas Drive

The original 123 acres of Alapocas Woods Park, now 145 acres, were deeded to Wilmington in 1910 by William Poole Bancroft, founder of the city's park system. The feature walk is the *Alapocas Nature Trail*, a 1.8-mile circuit of wide dirt trails and tumbling terrain above the Brandywine River. Look for majestic native trees in the airy woodland. Unmarked trails lead down to the Brandywine and a waterside trail past the most dramatic granite cliffs remaining along the river. The Brandywine Granite Company quarried over 600,000 tons of stone from this site between 1883 and 1888.

Awbury Arboretum

Philadelphia
Philadelphia County
Washington Lane between Chew Avenue and Ardleigh Street

Awbury Arboretum in East Germantown was the summer estate of 19th century Quaker shipping merchant Henry Cope. Across the 55 acres are plantings of groves and clusters of trees set amidst large swaths of grass fields in the English landscape garden tradition. You can investigate more than 200 species, mostly native, in your informal explorations of the grounds. Old macadam paths lead to most areas of the odd-shaped property. Also on the grounds are wetlands surrounding an artificial pond.

Banning Park
Wilmington
New Castle County
at the intersection of Maryland Avenue (Route 4) and Boxwood Road

The trails in the wooded area of this heavily used urban recreational park can take up to an hour to cover completely. The dirt trails are not marked and not mapped. Expect to pop out from the woods at a park boundary and retrace your steps as you explore these well-worn paths. The dog can cool off in two small ponds - Lewis Pond and the vegetation-choked Follies Pond.

Battery Park
New Castle
New Castle County
parking lot for park is on Third Street but can be accessed from many points in town

The paved trail leads away from the historic Colonial town of New Castle out of Battery Park for 1.25 miles (when not under construction). In addition to the long vistas across the Delaware River, there are some interesting marsh views on the opposite side of the trail as well. When the main *River Walk* reaches its terminus, you can continue on a narrow dirt trail that leads to a small rocky beach where your dog can jump into the Delaware. Along the way are small sandy beaches for your dog to play and some frisky waves at high tide.

Bear Swamp

Red Lion
Burlington County
Hawkins Road off Route 206 south of Route 70

A labyrinth of unmarked and unmaintained trails provide access to hundreds of protected acres of mixed hardwoods and pine trees. The soft dirt and sand trails are generally wide but there are places that will require bushwhacking and picking your way through muddy low spots. Look for trails leading into the woods on the north side of Hawkins Road, that switches from a macadam to dirt surface in the region of Bear Swamp. One such entrance is on the east side of a small bridge across Little Creek on the western edge of the hard surface/soft surface switchover.

Benjamin Rush State Park

Philadelphia
Philadelphia County
Roosevelt Boulevard (Route 1), just north of Southampton/Byberry Road
(must enter heading north on Route 1)

Benjamin Rush State Park was created in 1975 to honor the influential patriot Dr. Rush, chief physician for the Continental Army, but no funds were ever allocated for its development. The 275 acres of the Rush homestead became a favorite area for illegal dumping. Still undeveloped, the park's primary attractions are a model airplane field and community gardens rented and tended by local residents. Park near the gardens and begin hiking through the adjacent woods. Trails lead down to the gentle Poquessing Creek that occasionally bursts into pools deep enough for canine swimming. The informal network of trails sometimes travel on top of overgrown concrete drives and walks. The trails connect with more hiking in Poquessing Creek Park.

Berlin Park

Berlin
Camden County
between White Horse Pike, New Freedom Road and Park Drive

Several miles of densely wooded trails course through the park behind the Environmental Studies Center at the corner of Broad Street and Park Drive. The main pathway through the spine of the park is wide and composed of pebbly sand; it runs alongside the Great Egg Harbor River. Designated a Wild and Scenic River, the Great Egg Harbor is narrow, dark and forboding. Unmarked dirt trails branch from the trunk in narrow slivers through the thick woods. Also available is a short nature loop inside a wired path.

Black Rock Preserve

Phoenixville
Chester County
northeast of town on Route 113

Occupying 133 acres on a thumb of land where the Schuylkill River bends back on itself, the Black Rock Preserve has recently been developed. Molded hillsides and rocky waterfalls have been sculpted around an impoundment marsh. The red-stone trail of nearly one mile connects interpretive kiosks scattered about the wetlands. Down by the Schuylkill River an unmarked linear dirt trail hugs the river for nearly a mile and continues for another mile outside the preserve below Black Rock Dam, a stone-filled timber crib structure 11 feet high and 370 feet long. There is excellent access to the river from this flat trail (stay clear of the dam) for a canine aquatic workout.

Brandywine Springs Park

Marshallton
New Castle County
on Faulkland Road (Route 34) at the corner of
Newport Gap Pike (Route 41)

One of the first resort hotel-and-spas in America was built here in 1827. Later a popular amusement park evolved on the property, drawing thousands of funseekers to try an early version of a rollercoaster and other rides. Some remains of the park can still be seen along the trails. Kiosks housing turn-of-the 20th century photographs help recreate its heyday as a pioneering recreational site. There are walks in the upper region of the park, given over to picnic pavillions and ballfields while the lower, wooded section of the park, where the amusement rides were located, features blazed dirt trails. Look for the Wilmington & Western steam-powered tourist railroad to rumble across the open wooden trestle spanning Red Clay Creek.

Bringhurst Woods - Rockwood

Wilmington
New Castle County
off Carr Road, south of the Marsh Road Exit of I-95

A paved pathway, a link in the Northern Delaware Greenway, connects the woodlands of Bringhurst Woods with Rockwood, a unique rural Gothic estate built by 19th century merchant king Joseph Shipley. You will always seem to be walking up or down in these woods, but never laboriously. During the holiday season, the trees on the grounds of Rockwood are strung with thousands of lights making this lighted trail a must-visit destination. There are also dirt trails on the other side of Shellpot Creek but these are neither maintained nor enjoyable.

Brooke Farm Trail

Wayne
Delaware County
corner of Wayne Avenue and Maplewood Road

Radnor Township created this pleasing trail in woodlands suffocated by residential development. After a quick descent from the trailhead this short linear trail explores the bottomlands around the Little Darby Creek. The trail is well-blazed and wide. The Little Darby is an attractive waterway but not deep enough for more than splashing.

Central Perkiomen Valley Park

Perkiomenville
Montgomery County
Plank Road between Gravel Road (Route 29) and
Skippack Pike (Route 73)

Central Perkiomen Valley Park consists of 30 parcels of woodlands, open grass and wetlands hopscotching from Collegeville to Perkiomenville. There are two walks at the 55-acre park headquarters on Plank Road. A pedestrian trail snakes along the Perkiomen Creek, although there are not many water views once you leave the bridge area. An old

Reading Railroad right-of-way has been converted into a trail along Plank Road. Both are very rocky under paw. The Perkiomen Creek is wide but shallow and a superb canine swimming hole.

Chesapeake & Delaware Canal
Wildlife Area

St. Georges
New Castle County
several access points from Route 9

The old dirt towpaths on either side of the Chesapeake & Delaware Canal, managed by the U.S. Army Corps of Engineers, provide wide, flat, easy-walking paths. There are also informal dirt trails along the length of the canal. The scenery never changes and you have to turn around and retrace your steps at some point. The shores of the 40-foot deep channel are lined with boulders and not designed for swimming - dogs or otherwise.

Clayton Park

Boothwyn
Delaware County
entrance is on Garnet Mine Road off Route 322

Clayton Park began life in 1957 as a 59-acre gift from Mrs. Nelson Clayton and is today, at 170 acres, Delaware County's largest park. Much of the park is given over to a golf course with limited hiking available. A short multi-use trail loops through the trees around the parking lot. It is shaded and pleasant and good for walking the dog and pushing the baby stroller. A narrow, scruffy nature trail winds through the beech/maple climax forest at the edge of the park. A small branch of the Green Creek runs along the multi-use trail.

Cobbs Creek Park/Morris Park

Philadelphia
Philadelphia County
Lansdowne Avenue and Haverford Avenue

In the northern section of West Philadelphia's Cobbs Creek Park, across Haverford Avenue, is a good hour's worth of exploring in the woods of Morris Park. Trailheads are not marked so enter though openings in the woods and keep your eyes peeled for small orange dots on trees. This orange dot trail will take you on a rolling journey with occasional steep climbs through 200-year old trees and across two branches of Indian Creek as the streams flow towards Cobbs Creek, home of America's first water-powered mill. Highlights include a waterfall at a dramatic outcropping on the West Branch and the rock cliff of an abandoned stone quarry.

Core Creek Park

Langhorne
Bucks County
east of Route 413 off Tollgate Road or Bridgeton Pike

Core Creek is a busy recreational park developed on more than 1000 acres around Lake Luxemborg. Between breaks in the activity on the athletic fields and playgrounds there are patches of woods crossed by narrow dirt trails and wider bridle paths. A paved bicycle path is also available for dog walking. Lake Luxemborg is one of the best places in Bucks County to take the dog for a swim.

Curtis Arboretum

Wyncote
Montgomery County
on Church Road, just north of Township Line Road

The grounds of the former estate of *The Ladies Home Journal* publisher Cyrus H.K. Curtis are a popular spot for romping with your dog. There are no formal trails through Curtis Arboretum but if the informal dirt and grass paths are wet, you can walk on paved driveways. Although the current maintenance budget allows for little more than grass-cutting, hundreds of spectacular trees imported by Curtis from around the world remain. Two small ornamental ponds afford a quick doggie dip.

Delcastle Recreation Area
Wilmington
New Castle County
on McKennans Church Road between Limestone Road (Route 7) and
Newport Gap Pike (Route 41)

This multi-use recreation center offers a 1 3/4-mile paved circumference trail. If you are looking to commune with nature and not people, Delcastle is not for you. You will be sharing this busy pathway at any time of the day with joggers, in-line skaters, bicyclists and other dog walkers. There is no water in the park that doesn't come out of a fountain.

Diamond Rock Preserve
Devault
Chester County
on Chautauqua Trail off Howells Road

Diamond Rock Preserve, which includes a segment of the *Horse-Shoe Trail*, is a tract of land squeezed between the Pennsylvania Turnpike and emerging housing developments, managed by the Open Land Conservancy. The wooded preserve offers some interesting topography but there is always a feeling of walking in someone's backyard in the small preserve. There is not a drop of water at Diamond Rock Preserve.

Exton Park/Chester Valley Trail
Exton
Chester County
Route 30, behind the Church Farm School

In June 1994, Chester County and West Whiteland Township combined to jointly purchase 727 acres of land in heavily developed eastern Chester County. Together they will develop a park on the site. Available now is the initial one-mile segment of the proposed 16-mile bike-and-hike *Chester Valley Trail* between Downingtown and Norristown. The crushed stone and dirt path is cut through an open field and offers little shade for a four-legged friend.

Fisher Park

Philadelphia
Philadelphia County
Spencer and 5th Street

This neighborhood park in the Olney section features a network of wooded trails, offering about 1/2 hour of hiking. The narrow dirt trails radiate from a central sidewalk that bisects the park. A series of stone steps lead to the trails. The terrain is rolling and there is no water available. A small open field for romping with the dogs is also located in Fisher Park.

Fonthill

Doylestown
Bucks County
at Swamp Road and E. Court Street, 1/2 mile east of Route 611

Fonthill is the concrete castle - illuminated by more than 200 windows - built by Dr. Henry Chapman Mercer. Nearby is his Moravian Pottery and Tile Works where world-famous decorative tiles were crafted. Dog walkers can wander around the grounds and use the wide dirt trails through the woodlands on the estate. There is less than an hour of pleasant dog-walking here.

Fort DuPont State Park

Delaware City
New Castle County
entrance is off Route 9 behind the Governor Bacon Health Center

Fort DuPont, named for Civil War fleet commander Admiral Samuel Francis duPont, saw active duty in three wars before becoming a state park. The 1-mile *River View Trail*, a grassy loop path, begins in the marshland along the Delaware River and finishes in shaded woodlands. The trail takes you past several ruins of the military installation, camoflauged to river traffic, and features sustained views of the Delaware River and Fort Delaware on Pea Patch Island. There is no easy access to the water.

Fort Washington State Park

Flourtown
Montgomery County
turn onto Joshua Road from Skippack Pike (Route 73)
to entrance on left

The 493-acre park is named for a defensive redoubt built on this site by a regrouping Continental Army after a demoralizing defeat at Germantown in 1777. There are 3.5 miles of wooded trails in Fort Washington State Park, primarily in the Militia Hill Day Use Area. The interlocking trails, many on old vehicle roads, can be combined to form loop walks. The trails across Joshua Road are hilly; the grass and dirt cross-country trail that circumnavigates the picnic area less so. There is limited access to a deep stretch of the Wissahickon Creek at the edge of the park.

Four Mills Nature Reserve

Ambler
Montgomery County
the reserve is south of town at 12 Morris Road, east of Butler Pike

The Four Mills Nature Reserve comprises 55 acres of Wissahickon Creek floodplain. The trails at Four Mills lie on islands in the Wissahickon (if your dog shies away from open-grate bridges, you may need to carry him). A good linear walk here is to take the *Green Ribbon Trail* between water crossings upstream and downstream. There is less than an hour of hiking on the flat, soft dirt trails. The normal level of the Wissahickon Creek is not deep enough for dog paddling. Four Mills derives its name from four long-vanished mills that once operated in the vicinity.

Franklin Delano Roosevelt Park

Philadelphia
Philadelphia County
entrance on Pattison Street at intersection with Broad Street

Free yourself from a dependence on formal trails and you can cobble together quite an urban canine hike in this 348-acre greenspace in South Philadelphia. The park itself is a souvenir of the famous Olmsted brothers landscaping firm of the early 1900s and features classical elements and trademark serpentine pathways. The unique architecture of the American Swedish Historical Museum in the park is a blending of designs used in Swedish mansions and George Washington's Mount Vernon. The park is designed around Meadow Lake and features faint traces of a fresh water tidal marsh, an ecosystem nearly extinct in Pennsylvania.

Frosty Hollow Park

Levittown
Bucks County
the park is 1/4 mile east of Route 413 on New Falls Road

Much of the 95 acres of this shaded park are given over to tennis but there is a network of informal trails in the surrounding woodlands. These dirt trails are unmarked as they wind along and across Mill Creek, which is not deep enough for swimming. The walking in Frosty Hollow is level and easy.

Glen Providence Park

Media
Delaware County
in the western end of town at the end of State Street,
1 1/2 blocks off Baltimore Pike

This historic park was Delaware County's first, established in 1935 as the result of a gift of 30 acres from George Butler. There are a series of short linear trails in this wooded enclave. The trails do not loop and dead-end at park boundaries. After a steep slope away from the parking area, the unmarked trails are easy walking. The only water in Glen Providence Park is a shallow creek wandering from Broomall Lake to Ridley Creek.

Graeme Park

Horsham
Montgomery County
on County Line Road, just west of the intersection with Easton Road
(Route 611)

Graeme Park was built on 1200 acres in 1722 as the summer residence for the Provincial Governor of Pennsylvania, Sir William Keith. It is the only surviving residence of a Colonial Pennsylvania governor. Graeme Park features a quiet, 3/4-mile *Nature Trail*. Each of the 17 stops on the self-guided tour has been selected for its relevance to Colonial life in rural America. The soft grass and dirt path follows Park Creek for part of its journey, allowing a refreshing doggie dip.

Green Ribbon Trail

Montgomery County
there is access anywhere the trail crosses a public road

The *Green Ribbon Trail* is a linear trail in three segments along 21 miles of the Wissahickon Creek. The downstream segment is in Fairmount Park and the middle leg is a wooded band from Whitemarsh to Ambler. It gets less wooded in northern stretches from Pennlyn to North Wales. The walking is virtually always flat at creek level. The trailheads at public roads are marked by signposts and the trail is indicated by green blazes.

Hunsberger Woods

Collegeville
Montgomery County
off Route 29, south of Route 113

Collegeville Borough and the Montgomery Open Space Program, with the cooperation of the Hunsberger family, have preserved this narrow slice of land for permanent public use. The property features nice elevation changes on paw-friendly grass trails cut through fields and small groves of conifers. For canine refreshment a small stream with a millpond flows through the bottomlands. There can be nearly an hour of canine hiking here; look for an old springhouse off one trail.

Lake Towhee Park

Applebachsville
Bucks County
park is 1/4 mile east of town on Old Bethlehem Pike

An hour's hike will get you around 50-acre Lake Towhee but rarely will you glimpse the water. Low-lying stretches of the trail in the woods on the eastern side of the lake are all but impassable after heavy rains. The route is mostly flat with some minor climbs. Although the trail is marked with yellow dots the way becomes fuzzy through developed areas of the park.

Lenape Park/Menlo Park

Sellersville/Perkasie
Bucks County
the parks can be accessed from Route 152, Park Avenue East
or Constitution Avenue

Lenape Park is located on both sides of the East Branch Perkiomen Creek. The main walking track here is a paved bikeway alongside the creek that connects the 44 acres of the two parks. There is good access to the water for the dog but a high bank limits canine swimming in many places. An island in the creek is connected to the sides of the park by two lovely white suspension bridges. The South Perkasie Covered Bridge can be seen in Menlo Park.

Lower Perkiomen Valley County Park
Oaks
Montgomery County
just off Route 422 at Oaks/Audubon Exit on New Mill Road

Once the site of unprofitable copper mining operations, Lower Perkiomen Valley County Park is now a popular picnic spot. Dogs are not allowed in the picnic area but there are 30 acres of open multi-use fields in which dogs can romp. There is access to the deep Perkiomen Creek above the dam here.

New Brooklyn Park
New Brooklyn
Camden County
on New Brooklyn Road north of the Atlantic City Expressway
and east of Route 536

The park is the terminus of the Great Egg Harbor River where it feeds into New Brooklyn Lake. On the north shore of the lake there are unmarked trails and dirt roads in the woods of the 758-acre park. The trails are paw-friendly sand and dirt. A small sand beach offers access to the shallow waters of the 100-acre lake. A paved multi-purpose trail winds through the developed sections of the park.

Newlin Mill Park
Concordville
Delaware County
north of town on Route 1 at the intersection with South Cheyney Road

A park of 150 acres has been created where Nathaniel Newlin built a stone grist mill and dam on the headwaters of the West Branch of Chester Creek in 1704. The dirt and grass trail begins at the restored mill and once across the dam branches out for a tumbling walk of about three miles through woods and fields, including a Christmas tree nursery and a grove of California redwoods and sequoias that represent the three true cedars of the world. There is doggie dipping available in Chester Creek, especially behind the dam.especially behind the dam.

Oxford Valley Park

Fairless Hills
Bucks County
on Oxford Valley Road at intersection with Hood Boulevard

There are walking and biking trails through this slice of open space in busy Bristol Township. A paved trail goes most of the way around 9-acre Lake Caroline where the low banks of mown grass enable easy access for canine swimming. There are also some informal dirt trails through small woodlands here.

Palmer Park

Skippack
Montgomery County
Heckler and Creamery roads

Paved walking trails wind around and through recreation activities on the 55-acre swath of open space. The asphalt curves rise above their many brethren when they cut through a section of wetlands that has been left undisturbed. Grassy shoulders in the reeds give your dog a chance to walk on a soft surface. There is little shade along these paths.

Perkiomen Trail

Montgomery County
southern terminus in Valley Forge National Historic Park
and northern terminus in Green Lane Park

The entire *Perkiomen Trail* covers 22 miles as it follows an abandoned railbed along the Perkiomen Creek. Canine hikers wanting to try the tree-lined path can best do so from one of the three county parks it connects - you will find poop bags at trail accesses. The surface is paved in the lower sections to grind away a few nails. There is canine swimming in the muddy Perkiomen.

"To err is human, to forgive, canine."
-Anonymous

Playwicki Farm

Middletown
Bucks County
the park is on Maple Road (Route 213)

Southampton Township has preserved 110 acres of open space, believed to be the site of the Lenape Village of Playwicki, mentioned in the writings of William Penn. Ceramics and other artifacts have been uncovered along the bottomlands of Turkey Run on the edge of the park. The primary trail is a pleasing curvilinear design that snakes for 1.1 miles up and down rolling terrain. The paved route is accented by boulders and ancient farm machinery.

Port Penn Wetlands Trail

Port Penn
New Castle County
Route 9 at the corner of Liberty and Market streets

Port Penn was named after William Penn when he stopped for a drink of water in either 1682 or 1699. Views from the 1.5-mile *Wetlands Trail* are too often obscured by green tunnels of towering swamp grass but the open marsh views are stunning. Don't follow the trail to the end as it is cut across stalks of reeds waiting to impale your dog's paws. Rather, take the road directly to town and begin a half-mile *Village Walk* through structures dating to pre-American Revolution days.

Prophecy Creek Park

Blue Bell
Montgomery County
205 Skippack Pike (Route 73), opposite Narcissa Road, west of Butler Pike

Once the site of the "Battle of Old Mill Run," a Revolutionary War cavalry skirmish, Prophecy Creek is a farm-turned park. Open for exploration are the estate grounds, featuring Prophecy Creek feeding tranquil millponds, and barn with a brick silo. Cross an open-grate, green metallic bridge to the back of the 86-acre property and you will find a paw-friendly grass walking loop around an old field.

Rancocas State Park

Mount Holly
Burlington County
from the Mount Holly Bypass go west on Marne Highway (Route 537)
and make first right on Deacon Road to end after 1.3 miles

A tangle of unmarked paths and sand roads provide access to more than 1,200 acres of hardwood forest along the North Branch of the Rancocas Creek. The walking is mostly flat on soft dirt and sand. A portion of the park is leased to the Powhattan Indians who have occupied the land for hundreds of years. Dogs are not allowed on the trails of the Rancocas Nature Center.

Ringing Rocks Park

Upper Black Eddy
Bucks County
2 miles west of town on Ringing Rock Road

This park features two outstanding attractions: the highest waterfall in Bucks County and a boulder field of volcanic rocks. Their metallic bands stressed by several ice ages, the boulders produce a ringing sound when struck by a metal object. Short, wide trails lead through the woods to the boulder field and, beyond, to the waterfall.

River Park/Riverfront Park

Pottstown
Montgomery County
Hanover Street at the Schuylkill River

Riverfront Park features a 3/4 mile multi-use trail along the Schuylkill River. Unlike longer such trails, the pace here is more leisurely and well-suited for dog walking. Across the river in Chester County's River Park is an unmaintained trail which also parallels the river. The Riverfront Park trail is paved and includes wooden boardwalk bridges. The River Park trail is dirt; mud in wet times. There is abundant access to canine swimming in the Schuylkill River in these parks.

Rolling Hill Park

Gladwyne
Montgomery County
Rose Glen Road off Youngs Ford Road and Route 23

In the early 1990s, a small band of like-minded conservationists began gathering in a church basement to plot the preservation of Lower Merion's natural areas. Their first victory was the conversion of the former Walter C. Pew estate into the 103-acre Rolling Hill Park. Plans for formal trails and signage are still   incubating, so come with a mind to explore. The heavily wooded trails, some of which double as steeplechase practice routes, are generally wide and the terrain of the Mill Creek valley is hilly. There are some excellent stone house ruins deep in the woods along the trail.

Rose Tree Park

Media
Delaware County
entrance is on Providence Road (Route 252)

The Rose Tree Hunt Club, the oldest continuous fox-hunt club in America, first met here in 1859. A century later the Club's hunting range was so drastically reduced that they staged their last meet on April 9, 1964 and departed to York County. With only informal trails across the 120 acres of wide, rolling hills this is a park more for romping with the dog than channeling down predetermined routes. A small wooded glen, carved by a branch of Crum Creek, in the center of the park features shaded dirt trails.

Sandy Hollow Heritage Park
Birmingham
Chester County
South New Street between Birmingham Road and Thornbury Road

The Battle of the Brandywine was the largest battle of the American Revolution, spreading across ten square miles. As such it is difficult to interpret and the Brandywine Battlefield State Park is only 50 acres with no hiking (although a good place to take the dog for a game of fetch). Nearby, at the site of desperate fighting between Lord Cornwallis's British troops and Nathanael Greene's brigade on September 11, 1777, another 50 acres has been spared from development. A paved loop of about one mile tours the open field (there is no water here so bring some for your dog on a hot day). Look for a cannon along the left side that is pointed towards the scene of the most intense action. The Marquis de Lafayette was wounded in the thigh rallying American troops nearby and was treated at neighboring Bennett Farm.

Skunk Hollow
Newtown Square
Delaware County
parking on Saw Mill Road off Darby Paoli Pike

The Skunk Hollow trails were developed by Radnor Township to connect Saw Mill Park and The Willows. No dogs are allowed in either of these parks so don't continue past the terminals of these trails. The *Saw Mill* (yellow) and *Skunk Hollow* (white) trails flank the Little Darby Creek. Both are heavily wooded. There are some sporty climbs in Skunk Hollow on the well maintained dirt trails but contain a dispiriting number of root knobs, tiny tree stumps and exposed rocks.

Skymount Open Space

Tylersport
Montgomery County
Long Road off White's Mill Road

The only trail at Skymount Lake is an unmarked path cut through the grass about half way around the lake. The trailhead is also not marked: to pick it up walk down to the lake and turn right into the tall grass. There are ankle-eating holes in this mercifully short stretch of trail. The main attraction at Skymount for dog owners is the swimming in the lake.

Smedley Park

Springfield
Delaware County
Paper Mill Road off Baltimore Pike

There are two main trails in Smedley Park, blazed in red and yellow (a part of the *Springfield Trail*). Also available is the *Smedley-Leiper Trail*, opened in 1992. Frequented by runners, cyclists and rollerbladers, the paved path runs two miles to Leiper Park, former home of Thomas Leiper. This location, hard by the Blue Route, is hilly although none of the climbs is particularly harsh. Only the stretch of trail along the Crum Creek through the picnic area is flat. The hard surfaces of some of the park's trails encourage the breaking of bottles and threaten a pet's paws.

Robert G. Struble Hike-Bike Trail

Downingtown
Chester County
Norwood Road off Route 282 and Route 30

Created from an abandoned Pennsylvania Railroad line in 1979, the 10-foot wide multi-use *Struble Trail* will eventually connect Downingtown with Honey Brook Borough. Currently, 2.5 of the proposed 16 miles are completed. The crushed stone trail topped with oil is named for Robert Struble, a noted Chester County conservationist. The wooded trail shadows the East Branch of the Brandywine Creek for most of its route. Another paved spur leads to Jones Pond and Dowlin Forge Park.

Tacony Creek Park

Philadelphia
Philadelphia County
Adams Avenue, Rising Sun Avenue & Roosevelt Boulevard

The slender 302-acre Tacony Creek Park runs along the banks of the Tacony Creek (called Tookany in adjacent Montgomery County) for about 4 miles. A paved multi-purpose trail runs along the south shore with more trail options available south of Roosevelt Boulevard. The Tacony Creek is deep enough for dog paddling, especially near old dams on the water.

Timber Creek Park

Almonesson
Gloucester County
on the southeast corner of Hurffville Roud (Route 41)
and Cooper Street/Almonesson Road

This small park offers an eyehook trail whose highlight is a view of the wetlands of the Big Timber Creek estuary, home to ducks, geese, herons and kingfishers. The wide, soft dirt and sand trails follow a rolling, wooded path along the slopes above the marsh. This pleasant stroll takes less than one half hour but there is more at the Old Pine Farm (end of Rankin Avenue).

Timber Top Farm

West Chester
Chester County
off Route 322 on the way to Downingtown
(turn into field marked by green sign opposite elementary school)

The battle for the preservation of Chester County open space can be viewed from this loop trail at Timber Top Farm. The trail rambles for almost two miles around rolling farm fields that push back encroaching development. There is no water on this canine hike and shade only when the corn is high. Do not leave the trail - marked by metallic directional signs - since everything but the path is private property.

Upper Frederick Open Space
Frederick
Montgomery County
Colonial Road off Route 73 at Swamp Creek

This open space along Swamp Creek has been set aside by Upper Frederick Township. There are two markedly different linear trails here; downstream is a creekside walk through marshy bottomland and upstream is a sensuous, rolling trail through a grove of Eastern hemlock, the Pennsylvania state tree. There are good swimming holes in Swamp Creek, along which grows a species of hickory tree bearing nuts of extraordinary size in a hard, thick shell.

Valley Creek Preserve
Devault
Chester County
Tree Line Road off Valley Road

There is one linear trail that traverses these lowlands dominated by the meanderings of the Valley Creek. When the vegetation is heavy the path can be quite narrow and the dirt and grass trail can become impassable after a heavy rain. The pretty Valley Creek is not consistently deep enough for sustained doggie dips but you will be hard-pressed to keep water-loving dogs on its banks.

Valley Garden Park
Greenville
New Castle County
on Campbell Road (Route 82) off Kennett Pike (Route 52)

An ideal spot for a picnic with the dog, the main walking trail is a sloping 15-minute loop around a tumbling brook. You can also explore the netherlands of the park that consists of peaceful fields and small stands of woods. The main paths are paved; once off the loop the walking is mostly on grass. The brook is not deep enough for dog-paddling.

West Deptford Park

Woodbury
Gloucester County
from Exit 20 of I-295, east on Mid Atlantic Parkway
to Metropolitan Road

A long paved loop encircles this athletic complex on the edge of the woods. The trail is flat most of the way around. There is no water available in the park. Doggie poop bags are provided for the dog walkers.

West Valley Nature Area

East Bradford
Chester County
at the corner of Downingtown Pike (Route 322) and Skelp Level Road

The West Chester Fish, Game and Wildlife Association created this 70-acre nature preserve for walkers on PECO Energy land. The grass trail starts benignly past a small spring before winding rather sharply up a hillside through brushy understory to open meadows before returning to the parking lot. This is a short but energetic canine hike.

White Clay Creek State Park - Judge Morris Estate

Newark
New Castle County
Polly Drummond Road between Kirkwood Highway and Old Coach Road

This two-year old trail is one of the best loop hikes in the tri-state area. In about an hour the route twists across forested slopes, teeters above scenic streams and fords broad ravines. The dirt trail has been cut purposely narrow to reduce the impact on these pristine woods. There is one cut-off to shorten the main loop but don't shortchange yourself and the dog by taking it. Additional trails across the road connect with the Middle Run Natural Area (page 52).

White Clay Creek State Park - Possum Hill

Newark
New Castle County
off Paper Mill Road (Route 72), north of Possum Park Road

There are two connected walks here - the short 1.17-mile inner loop, blazed in blue, and the 2-mile *Long Loop*, blazed in red. The scenery on the Long Loop is more arresting with impressive displays of towering oak and beech trees but the *Short Loop* packs more surprises - an old hidden mill pond and a marker memorializing the base point of the Mason-Dixon Line. The terrain through fields and woodlands is easy to walk, save for one tough climb on the Long Loop.

How To Pet A Dog
Tickling tummies slowly and gently works wonders. Never use a rubbing motion; this makes dogs bad-tempered. A gentle tickle with the tips of the fingers is all that is necessary to induce calm in a dog. I hate strangers who go up to dogs with their hands held to the dog's nose, usually palm towards themselves. How does the dog know that the hand doesn't hold something horrid? The palm should always be shown to the dog and go straight down to between the dog's front legs and tickle gently with a soothing voice to acompany the action. Very often the dog raises its back leg in a scratching movement, it gets so much pleasure from this.
-Barbara Woodhouse

More Places To Take Your Dog In The Philadelphia Region...

Paws on The Road

Here are four short road trips that are sure to set tails wagging for adventurous canine hikers: one to the north (Ricketts Glen State Park); one to the east (Morristown National Historic Park); one to the south (Gunpowder Falls State Park) and one to the west (Nolde State Forest).

Ricketts Glen State Park

The Park:
One of the most uniquely scenic areas in the Northeast, Ricketts Glen was slated to become a national park in the 1930s but World War II shelved plans for this development. Instead, Ricketts Glen opened as a state park in 1944. Gradually the Commonwealth of Pennsylvania continued purchasing blocks of land from the descendents of Robert Bruce Ricketts until the park spread across more than 13,000 acres.

Ricketts enlisted as a private in the United States Army in 1861 and after commanding a battery during the Civil War was discharged with the rank of Colonel. When the war ended, Colonel Ricketts began acquiring inaccessible virgin timber and he would eventually control over 80,000 acres of land. His Central Penn Lumber Company began harvesting the old growth forest, with some trees 900 years old, when the railroads arrived in 1890. By 1913 the timber was exhausted and the lumber town of Ricketts deserted.

The Walks:
The spectacular attraction of Ricketts Glen is the magical *Falls Trail*, a Y-shaped exploration of 23-named waterfalls. Two branches of the Kitchen Creek slice through the Ganoga Glen to the left and Glen Leigh to the right before uniting at Waters Meet. The stem of the trail flows through Ricketts Glen, among towering hemlocks and oaks, before tumbling over three cascades at Adams Falls at the trailhead.

The remoteness of the land in the 19th century kept the waterfalls, ranging as high as the 94-foot Ganoga Falls, undiscovered until 1865. Colonel Ricketts hired a crew to build a trail along and across the plunging water and the project took 28 years. Today the *Falls Trail* remains a maintenance challenge and its steep grades can be muddy and slippery and your dog's four-wheel traction will be most welcome. The two prongs of the trail connect at the top of the twin falls via the 1.2-mile *Highland Trail*. The complete falls experience encompasses almost seven miles.

More than 20 miles of trails meander through the deep woods and mountain lakes at Ricketts Glen. The rocky *Cherry Run Trail* takes you away from the crowded Glens Natural Area into the eastern section of the park and the *Grand View Trail* is a 1.9-mile loop that reaches a fire tower with an almost complete 360-degree vista. Other less demanding trails mosey along near 245-acre Lake Jean.

Directions to Ricketts Glen State Park:

The park is 30 miles north of Bloomsburg. The main park entrance is off Route 487 between Red Rock and Dushore. A good way to reach the Falls Trail is to travel on Route 118, east of its intersection with Route 487, and park in the lot on the right for the *Evergreen Trail*.

Morristown National Historic Park

The Park:

Morristown, a village of 250, was a center of iron supply for the American Revolution and even though it lay only 30 miles west of the main British force in New York it was protected by a series of parallel mountain ranges. It was the twin luxuries of a defensible position and close proximity to the enemy that twice brought General George Washington to camp his main army here, first in 1777 and again in 1779-1780.

After the Battle of Princeton in January 3, 1777 a worn-down Washington's Colonial army swarmed the tiny town seeking shelter in the few public buildings, private homes, barns and stables then in existence. Steadily Washington rebuilt his flagging troops, overcoming desertion and insipient food shortages. His greatest foe, however, was disease. An outbreak of smallpox threatened to decimate the small army and Washington ordered the little known and, to many, horrifying procedure of innoc-ulation. Some indeed died but most of his troops did not contract the deadly pox.

The park was created in 1933 as America's first national historic park.

The Walks:

Canine hiking at Morristown National Historic Park is found at the Jockey Hollow Encampment Area. When here, nothing could have prepared the Continental Army for the worst winter of the 18th century. Twenty-eight blizzards pounded the slopes and whipped through the wooden huts that were cut from 600 acres of hardwood forests here.

Revolutionary War-era huts like this one are familiar to canine hikers in Valley Forge but this one is in Morristown.

The forest has grown back and is open and airy with long views through the trees from the trail. Four main trails circle the Jockey Hollow Encampment. The 6.5-mile *Grand Loop Trail,* blazed in white, circles the park but doesn't visit any historical attractions without a detour. It is also the only trail that cannot be accessed from the centrally located Trail Center.

The *Aqueduct Loop Trail* and the stacked loop *Primrose Brook Trail* are two of the prettiest rambles in the park as they trace some of the many gurgling streams that once attracted the Colonial Army.

All the junctions on the first-rate trails feature directional signs and park maps.

The long-distance *Patriot's Path* links Jockey Hollow to the New Jersey Encampment Area and neighboring parks and contributes mightily to the total of 27 well-groomed miles of Morristown trails.

Directions to Morristown National Historic Park:
Morristown is located along interstate 287 in New Jersey. Traveling south on 287, use exit 36; traveling north on 287, exit at 36A. Look for the signs for Jockey Hollow.

Gunpowder Falls State Park

The Park:
Gunpowder Falls State Park embraces more than 17,000 acres of Maryland countryside in six distinct tracts from the Pennsylvania border to the Chesapeake Bay. There are some 100 miles of trails in the park where the fall line of the Piedmont Plateau caused rivers (known as "falls" in Maryland) to tumble and generate abundant water power for colonial mills.

The Walks:
The easiest place for northerners to get to in Gunpowder Falls State Park is the Belair Section directly on Route 1, north of Baltimore. The best swimming for your dog in the park is here on Long Green Run, past the *Sweathouse Trail*, where a whale-shaped rock serves as a natural diving board for playful dogs. The trails run for eight miles along the Big Gunpowder Falls on both sides of Route 1. Away from the water chutes in the river there are healthy hill climbs and wide trails that give a big feel to this canine hike as it meanders through differing forest types.

Some of the best trails are in the Hereford section where the *Gunpowder South Trail* includes bites of trail more reminiscent of mountainous West Virginia than suburban Baltimore, especially from Falls Road to Prettyboy Dam. While most of the narrow dirt trails at Hereford are easy on the paw, this waterside path is rocky and requires a fair amount of scrambling. Your reward is stunning views of the rugged gorge.

Unlike other sections of the park the water is not the star at Sweet Air where upland farm fields, lush riparian forests and fern-encrusted hillsides are backdrops for canine hikes on the trail system along the Little Gunpowder Falls.

*The lush vegetation of the Hereford Section of Gunpowder Falls
State Park is like a visit to the jungle for your dog.*

Hiking at Jerusalem Mill is along both sides of the Little
Gunpowder Falls and downstream from the restored grain mill is
the Jericho Covered Bridge, one of only six remaining covered
bridges in Maryland.

Crowds are normally not a problem on the strung-out
park trails but near-complete solitude is achieved in the
Pleasantville section of Gunpowder Falls where the the trail
follows an abandoned railbed of the Maryland and Pennsylvania
Railroad, known affectionately as the Ma & Pa. It took the
peripatetic short-line railroad 77.2 twisting miles to cover its
49 -mile distance.

Canine hikers will want to avoid Dundee Creek where
dogs are banned from the Hammerman Day Use Area, although
there is quiet hiking with your dog here in the bullrushes along
Dundee Creek.

Directions to Gunpowder Falls State Park:

Park headquarters are located in Kingsville on Jerusalem
Mill Road off US 1. This is the only place to pick up trail maps
for the park; trailhead parking lots feature only a mapboard.
All trails in Gunpowder Falls State Park are well-blazed.

Nolde Forest

The Park:

Jacob Nolde arrived in Philadelphia as a 21-year old from Germany in 1880 and soon found himself among the German-speaking communities of Berks County. He found work as a weaver and within a decade had purchased enough knitting machines to start his own hosiery manufacturing business. In another ten years he had taken over an entire Reading city block and was operating the second largest textile plant in America.

Nolde now had the time and resources to pursue his dream: the establishment of a manicured, managed forest typical of his Bavarian homeland. He began by purchasing land where he discovered a single white pine tree growing in an abandoned meadow. The lone pine would soon be joined by more than a half-million neighbors - white pine, yellow pine, Norway spruce, Douglas fir, and other coniferous varieties - as Nolde sought to create "the most beautiful pine forest in Pennsylvania."

A small platform makes for an ideal canine diving board at a small pond int he Nolde Forest.

The Walks:

After passing out of the family, the Commonwealth of Pennsylvania now shepherds Jacob Nolde's dream on 665 pine-scented acres. There are some 10 miles of trails coursing through the forest, mostly on wide, former access roads built by the plantation's foresters. The well-spaced conifers indeed give the feeling of rambling through a pine farm in places.

The focal point for much of the canine hiking is Punches Run that flows energetically through the valley floor. Strict adherence to the trail system will roughly generate a figure-eight hike but chances are you will be tempted to break off your intended route to explore something interesting in the verdant forest.

Directions to Nolde Forest:

Nolde Forest is southwest of Reading on PA 625, two miles south of PA 724.

The swimming is easy in the Nolde Forest.

174

Dog Parks In
The Philadelphia
Region...

Dog Parks

Dog parks often begin as informal gatherings of dog owners that eventaully become legitimized by local government. A dog park can be a place for your dog to run off-leash or romp with other dogs or a chance for you to play with your dog in a friendly environment. Before ranking some Delaware Valley dog parks, here are some tips for enjoying your visit to the dog park:

- Keep an eye on your dog and a leash in hand. Situations can change quickly in a dog park.

- Keep puppies younger than 4 months at home until they have all necessary innoculations to allow them to play safely with other dogs. Make certain that your older dog is current on shots and has a valid license.

- ALWAYS clean up after your dog. Failure to pick up your dog's poop is the quickest way to spoil a dog park for every one.

- If your dog begins to play too rough, don't take time to sort out blame - leash the dog and leave immediately.

- Leave your female dog at home if she is in heat.

- Don't volunteer to bring all the dogs in the neighborhood with you when you go. Don't bring any more dogs than you can supervise comfortably.

- Observe and follow all posted regulations at the dog park.

- HAVE AS MUCH FUN AS YOUR DOG

Blue Ribbon - **Harford Dog Park** *(Delaware County: Denbigh Road, just east of junction of Gulph Creek Road and Biddulph Road)*

A large, grassy hillside has formally been given over to dogs with enough room for a half-dozen games of fetch. The space is unfenced and a small walking path working its way around most of the perimeter of the park visits several impressive mature trees. Gulph Creek gurgles past the back of the property to provide relief on a hot day, although it is not deep enough for extended canine aquatics. The drinking fountain, however, is built for humans and dogs. Poop bags are provided. Open daylight hours only.

There is plenty of room for dogs to explore at the Harford Dog Park.

#2 - **Carousel Bark Park** *(New Castle County: Limestone Road, Route 7, between Route 41 and Route 2)*

If your dog prefers to spend most of her play date in the water rather than on land, this is the dog park to choose. The off-leash area in Carousel Park borders a large lake with smooth banks to launch dogs for a dip. A large, unmown field serves as a gathering place. When your dog is through socializing take a hike across the rolling hills. Poop bags provided. Open during daylight hours.

There is plenty of room to swim and plenty of room to romp at Carousel Bark Park

#3 - **Orianna Hill Dog Park** *(Philadelphia County: in Northern Liberties on the 900 block of North Orianna Street, between 2nd and 3rd and Poplar and Wildey streets)*

By statute, it is illegal to have a dog off leash anywhere in Philadelphia, even if an area is so designated by park officials. A dog is not allowed to be off-leash on *any* public property. The Orianna Hill Dog Park is the only dog park owned by the residents and thus the only legal place to let your dog run off leash in the city. Alhough privately operated, guest dogs are welcome. The fenced-in area is large and graced with shade trees and gardens and plenty of personal touches like painted murals.

#4 - **Schuylkill River Park Dog Run** *(Philadelphia County: west end of park, opposite 25th & Spruce Street, next to community gardens)*

The standard for fenced-in urban dog parks, this is Philadelphia's premier Center City dog run. The fenced area, with two sections for large and small dogs, is 35 yards by 75 yards with a wood chip-and-dirt surface. There are some shade trees and six sturdy benches. The water fountain is built for people and dogs. The area is lit but not adequately enough for night use.

#5 - **Rockford Park** *(New Castle County: the city of Wilmington at 19th Street and Tower Road)*

A grassy field at the bottom of a sledding hill has been designated as an off-leash area, good for a game of fetch or a dog-gathering area. Poop bags are provided but you must bring your own water. Open during daylight areas.

#6 - **Montgomery Township Bark Park** *(Montgomery County: behind Bell Run Plaza in Lansdale on Route 63, west of Route 202)*

A short, curvilinear path leads out of the shopping center parking lot to this one-acre off-leash oasis. Enclosed with a chain-link fence, there is plenty of room for suburban dogs to romp here. Several large trees provide shade in the summer. Poop bags and trash cans are provided. Bring your own water in case the dog bowls have run dry. Open during daylight hours only.

Personal touches at the Montgomery Township Bark Park include plastic fire hydrants.

#7 - Cooper River Pooch Park *(Camden County: end of North Park Drive, in Cherry Hill)*

In the back of the park are two small dog runs, one for dogs more than 30 pounds and one for smaller dogs. There is no shade but a water fountain with bowl is available. The Pooch Park has lights and is open until 10:00 p.m.

#8 - "Duke's Dog Run" in Freedom Park *(Burlington County: in Medford at 86 Union Street, south of Route 70)*

Problems with uncontrolled dogs led to the loss of freedom in a 10-acre field of this park. But rather than banning dogs completely as some townships might have considered, Medford Township constructed a dog run instead. Leashes are mandatory right up to the gate.

#9 - Utilitarian Philadelphia neighborhood dog runs:
Mario Lanza Park at 214 Catherine Street in Bella Vista
SPOAC Dog Park at Passyunk and Dickinson streets in south Philadelphia

Your Dog At
The Beach...

Your Dog At The Beach

It is hard to imagine many places a dog is happier than at a beach. Whether running around on the sand, jumping in the water or just lying in the sun, every dog deserves a day at the beach. But all too often dog owners stopping at a sandy stretch of beach are met with signs designed to make hearts - human and canine alike - droop: NO DOGS ON BEACH. Below are rules for taking your dog on a day trip to one of our Atlantic Ocean beaches.

DELAWARE

Off-season, Delaware's quiet, sandy beaches area a paradise for dogs. Don't bother to make a special trip for the sparse Delaware Bay beaches.

Bethany Beach	No dogs on the beach or boardwalk from April 1 to October 1
Delaware Seashore State Park	Dogs are allowed on the beach from October 1 to May 1
Dewey Beach	Dogs are not allowed on the beach between 9:30 am to 5:30 pm in season
Fenwick Island	No dogs permitted on the beach from May 1 to September 30
Lewes/ Cape Henlopen	From May 1 to September 30 no dogs are allowed on the beach between 8:00 am and 6:30 pm
Rehoboth Beach	Dogs are prohibited from the beach and boardwalk from April 1 to October 31

MARYLAND

The drive is a little longer but if you want your dog to enjoy the ocean waves in the summer the place to go is Assateague Island National Seashore.

Assateague Island National Seashore	Dogs are allowed on the beach but not on the trails year-round
Assateague State Park	No dogs are allowed on the beach
Ocean City	Dogs are allowed on the beach and boardwalk October 1 to April 30

NEW JERSEY

In-season, the New Jersey shore isn't especially welcoming to canine hikers. After Labor Day, however, some of America's best sand beaches start to open wide for dogs.

Asbury Park	Dogs are allowed on beach in off-season
Atlantic City	Dogs are not permitted on the beaches or boardwalk anytime
Avalon	Dogs are not permitted on the beach, boardwalk or dunes between March 1 and September 30
Avon-By-The-Sea	Dogs allowed on beach from November 1 to April 1 but never on the boardwalk
Barnegat Light	Dogs are prohibited from May 1 to October 1
Beach Haven	No dogs allowed on the beach
Belmar	Dogs are not allowed on the beach year-round
Bradley Beach	Dogs are allowed from October 15 to April 15

Brigantine	Dogs are allowed on the beach from 14th Street north to the northernmost jetty
Cape May	Dogs are not allowed on the beach, board walk or outdoor shopping areas
Cape May Point	No dogs allowed on the beach
Gateway National Recreation Area - Sandy Hook	Dogs allowed on the beach from Labor Day to March 15

You never know what treasure will wash ashore on a beach, like this coconut at Gateway National Recreation Area.

A Bark In The Park -

The 55 Best Places To Hike With Your Dog In The Philadelphia Region

DOUG GELBERT

illustrations by

ANDREW CHESWORTH

Cruden Bay Books

There is always a new trail to look forward to...

A BARK IN THE PARK: THE 55 BEST PLACES TO HIKE WITH
YOUR DOG IN THE PHILADELPHIA REGION (2nd Edition)

Cruden Bay Books
PO Box 467
Montchanin, DE 19710
www.hikewithyourdog.com

International Standard Book Number 0-9744083-4-4

Manufactured in the United States of America

Island Beach State Park	Dogs are not allowed in recreational areas but have access to other beaches any time of the year
Lavallette	No dogs allowed on beach but can go on boardwalk after Labor Day
Mantoloking	Dogs allowed on the beach October 1 to May 15 anytime; otherwise dogs allowed from sunrise to 8 AM and 6 PM to sunset

Sometimes good sticks are hard to find on the open dunes of Island Beach State Park.

North Wildwood	Dogs are not allowed on the beach from May 15 to September 15
Ocean City	Dogs are never allowed on the boardwalk but can be leashed on the beach from October 1 to April 30
Ocean Grove	Dogs are permitted on the beach and boardwalk from October 1 to May 1

Point Pleasant	Dogs are allowed anytime from September 15 until June 15; before 8:00 AM and after 6:00 PM in the summer
Sea Isle City	No dogs are permitted on the beach, beach approaches or promenade at any time
Ship Bottom	No dogs allowed on the beach until October 1
Spring Lake	Dogs are allowed on the beach in the off-season
Stone Harbor	No dogs allowed on the beach, boardwalk or dunes anytime between March 1 and September 30
Surf City	No dogs allowed on the beach
Wildwood	No dogs allowed on the beach
Wildwood Crest	No animals of any kind allowed on the beach

Active dogs are never at a loss for things to do at the beach.

Tips For Taking Your Dog To The Beach

- The majority of dogs can swim and love it, but dogs entering the water for the first time should be tested; never throw a dog into the water. Start in shallow water and call your dog's name - or try to coax him in with a treat or toy. Always keep your dog within reach.

- Another way to introduce your dog to the water is with a dog that already swims and is friendly with your dog. Let your dog follow his friend.

- If your dog begins to doggie paddle with his front legs only, lift his hind legs and help him float. He should quickly catch on and will keep his back end up.

- Swimming is a great form of exercise, but don't let your dog overdo it. He will be using new muscles and may tire quickly.

- Be careful of strong tides that are hazardous for even the best swimmers.

- Cool ocean water is tempting to your dog. Do not allow him to drink too much sea water. Salt in the water will make him sick. Salt and other minerals found in the ocean can damage your dog's coat so regular bathing is essential.

- Check with a lifeguard for daily water conditions - dogs are easy targets for jellyfish and sea lice.

- Dogs can get sunburned, especially short-haired dogs and ones with pink skin and white hair. Limit your dog's exposure when the sun is strong and apply sunblock to his ears and nose 30 minutes before going outside.

- If your dog is out of shape, don't encourage him to run on the sand, which is strenuous exercise and a dog that is out of shape can easily pull a tendon or ligament.

Canine Hiking Clubs

Dogs naturally like to run in packs and their people are also discovering the joys of hiking in groups. One local hiking group organizes outings specifically with their canine companions in mind - the Chester County Canine Hiking Club.

A canine hiking group is a good way to socialize your dog and learn the ways of the trail. The Chester County Canine Hikers pack often includes puppies and veteran trail sniffers. Most hikes last between an hour and 90 minutes and destinations are often selected with a good swimming hole in mind.

Any non-aggressive dog is welcome and be certain to bring a poop bag to keep parks clean. In fact, the club holds special hikes throughout the year to do trail maintenace.

For information on joining the Chester County Canine Hiking Club you can check out their website via a link at www.hikewithyourdog.com.

Index To Parks...

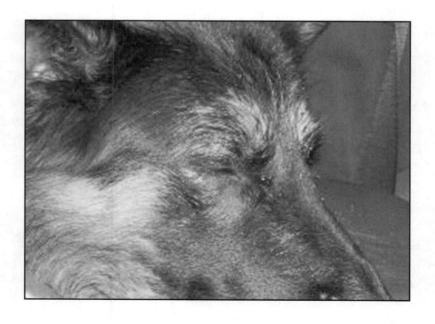